o Ernesto Lópe

Gracias por tod

ijro cuenta un poco de nuestra

historia.

We Are Not
Born Failures

Con Amor

Moisés Linares

Cover design by Steve Alfaro
Cover photo by Khristian Garay
Photos provided by Moisés Linares, Khristian Garay, Omar Garcia & APS (All Pro Sports)
Editors: Veronica Gonzales & Kaytie Bishop

Published in the United States by RIA JAY Publishing
3355 Lenox Road Suite 750 Atlanta, GA 30326
www.riajay.com

ISBN 978-1-955727-02-0 (Paperback)
Printed in the United States of America First printing
October 2021

Dedication

This book is dedicated to my mother who sacrificed everything for me to have an opportunity to succeed. A woman who worked as a housekeeper and street vendor in order to put food on our table. She showed me the true meaning of strength and not be ashamed of hard and honest work. Because of you, I can say I've made the best of my opportunities while being authentic and vulnerable.

I also dedicate this book to my grandmother the matriarch of our family who ignited a fire that pushed me to finish this book. I know she's rejoicing knowing I fulfilled the promise I made many years ago. For my cousin Josue who passed away due to Covid-19 in April of 2020. You were my brother from another mother and one of my biggest supporters who always felt proud of the work I did. I love you bro.

To my team and friends Khristian Garay, Steve Alfaro, Veronica Gonzales, Josue Guajan, Juosseef Alba, Roberto Gonzalez and Omar Garcia, this book came to life with your help. It's a true testament that it takes a great team to create something special. South Central Los Angeles, this is for you. I learned the meaning of grit growing up in the streets and playing sports in some of the toughest neighborhoods around the city. Now I can stand up tall and tell people all over the country and world that we can accomplish anything regardless of where you are from.

Thank You,

Moisés

We Are Not Born Failures

Do not judge me by my successes; judge me by how many times I fell down and got back up again. — Nelson Mandela

Gramercy place between Slauson and 54th street in South Los Angeles.

There are moments in life that transform us. They have the ability to shape who we become. These instances result from the hardships and pain we experience, often revealing a strength within us that we never realized was there. If you pay close attention during these times, you can dig in and find your purpose. My moment was in the 10th grade.

It was a regular day, just like any other. I got off the bus at my usual stop on Western and 57th, like I always did after my hour-long commute home from soccer practice. Following my five-block walk, I rounded the corner onto my street and immediately noticed something was wrong. I strained my eyes trying to make sense of the scene on my front lawn. With every step I took, my pace dramatically slowed down. I felt my chest tightening and a pinch in my heart that told me something was terribly wrong.

As I moved closer, things became clear. The old black sofas my mom had worked so hard to purchase were outside, abandoned.

7

I touched the weathered leather while surveying the area in disbelief. Shards of glass slipped through my fingers and fell to the ground as I picked up a shattered picture frame. In it contained a special family photo— one of the only photos we had taken together. The photo that was once proudly on display in our living room was now tossed aside like it meant nothing.

A short distance away I spotted my #10 soccer club jersey lumped on top of a dresser. All of our belongings were scattered across the lawn of our duplex— furniture, clothing, television, you name it. My family's entire existence was spread out for everyone to see, and the contents of our lives were no longer inside those four walls. We had been evicted.

I walked among our memories, looking for my mother and sisters. There was an eerie silence that felt thick around me. In shock, I sat on the front porch as tears welled up in my eyes. Teardrops rolled down my cheeks and fell to the ground, reminiscent of the shards of glass that fell from the broken frame. My heart was heavy. My family was gone. I had no idea where they were, and I had no idea what was to happen next.

My mother, grandmother, and siblings during abuela Rosa Emília's birthday celebration.

Soon, the afternoon turned into early evening, and the streetlights dimmed as darkness took over. I looked down to see a soccer ball at my feet. It gave me some comfort, and I carried it with me as I attempted to search for my family. Soccer was the one thing that was constant for me, and it taught me discipline and teamwork. At that moment, it felt like that ball was my only friend. It was a symbol of something that had carried me through difficult times and, once again, showed up when I needed it the most.

After searching and not finding anything, I returned to the stoop. I rolled the ball back and forth in front of me, trying to collect my thoughts. Where would I sleep for the night? Was my family safe? Where would we live? Would I go back to school? What next? It was not the first time we had been without a home, and it was hard to shake the "here we go again" thoughts as they entered my mind with sinking discouragement.

Deep down, I knew it was only a matter of time before we needed to leave that place we called, home. My mother, stepfather, sisters, and I had been living there rent-free for years. Two years after we moved in, the property had gone to foreclosure. For months, we waited for someone to arrive and tell us what was would happen next. We figured we would either be told to leave or have the option to rent from the new owner. No one ever came, so we decided to stay and ride the wave. Five years later, we finally got our answer.

I searched for the blessing in the apparent eviction.

A Knock, Years in the Making

Although our eviction is in the distant past, that dreadful event is something that will never be forgotten. My mother and sisters recall that day so clearly. It was early morning, not long after I had left for school, that the Los Angeles Sheriff's Department rapidly knocked on our door. My mother had been in the kitchen, preparing *cereal con leche* for breakfast, when the knock reverberated through the darkness of early morning. Upon entering they ordered that my family collect all of our belongings and vacate the home immediately. Amongst their demands, they shouted for my mother and sisters to grab their things and move quickly. My 11-year-old sister, Jennifer, remembered that it was still dark outside. My sisters, Karla and Jennifer, were just waking up, still rubbing sleep from their eyes. Everyone was taken by surprise. Quickly, they shook their lethargy and grabbed for whatever items they could carry. Unable to collect everything, many items were left behind.

My sisters were terrified with every harsh reminder from the sheriff's officers to keep moving. Karla and Jennifer recalled the silence in the house in between their commands. Quiet hung in the air, thick and heavy from the weight of current events. My sisters looked to my mother, searching for answers, and waited for direction. She did not say a word. Limited in her English despite having been in the United States for almost twenty years, my mother didn't understand the totality of what was happening. She couldn't fully understand what the sheriffs were telling her.

The officers insisted we had known about the eviction date. They repeated that my family needed to pick up the pace and leave our home. They kept referencing a letter that was sent to our home weeks before through the mail. The reiteration of 'the letter' confused everyone, even my sisters, who could more clearly understand the officers than my mother. No one had seen any letter. No one except my stepfather, who had hidden the said letter from everyone.

While I spent my day in school, ignorant of the pain flooding my childhood home, my sisters were in tears on our front lawn as my mother hugged and consoled them. She pieced together the morning's events and was now boiling with rage. My stepfather, Carlos, had intercepted the eviction notice — 'the letter' — allowing her to be blindsided by the knock at the door.

As the morning of the eviction carried on, the people on our street began leaving their homes for work. With pity and confusion, our neighbors quickly turned a blind eye to the sheriff's car and the tragedy unfolding on our lawn. Many of these people had known our family for years and would often attend our birthday celebrations and our BBQs. They were not just our neighbors, but friends and extended family with whom we had formed close relationships with. My mother steered my sisters to walk with her through the back alley to avoid the glances in order to grieve in solitude. She felt humiliated and betrayed.

The alley behind the duplex led past our backyard, where my sisters and mother discovered Carlos, passed out again from another long night of drinking. My mother's anguish quickly turned into anger. She roused him awake and, looking into his bloodshot eyes, she blamed him for disrupting our lives and uprooting us from our family home. She remained calm but firm in her words. Carlos, never a humble nor passive man, climbed to his knees and begged for forgiveness. He realized that her tolerance for him had run out.

That morning was the last time we were all together in the same place as a family.

Carlos was the biological father of my sisters (Ingrid, Karla, Jennifer, and Elkhen). He was a Christian pastor and for flashes of our childhood, we experienced him as a leader, teacher, and a good father. He taught us discipline and pushed us in the direction of righteousness. Our family was in church five out of the seven days of the week, praying and praising God for all the good things we had in our life. I even remember quality time during family dinners, taking trips to the beach, and hiking together. Howver, Carlos had a darker side. One that brought

11

out bipolar tendencies, quickly changing his moods from one end to another. His vice was alcohol.

Though Carlos had issues expressing any type of emotion, he would often talk about us about his rough upbringing in Honduras. He recalled being a teen and finding out that his father had been brutally murdered and told us about the lack of love he received as a child. With bottled-up resentment and pain from the life he left behind, he would often lash out in violent fits of rage. Though he turned to alcohol as a coping mechanism, it did more harm than good. His alcohol abuse led him to sporadically leave the church and often our family.

When Carlos was not aligned in faith and with the church, he was an abusive drunk, triggered by the slightest interruptions of his day. His drinking knew no limitations. We grew accustomed to having an angry drunk in our home. I was five years old the first time I saw him beat my mother in a drunken rage. My mother had returned home from the grocery store with baby formula for my sister Karla, then a newborn. Carlos greeted us at the door, angry that my mother had decided to leave Karla home with him. As he yelled at my mother, I began to cry, and he locked me into my highchair to beat my mother without distraction. Carlos slapped, punched, and pushed my mother until she became a small ball on the floor. He eventually grew weary from his punches and left the house in our station wagon. That day, he would head back to Honduras for a few years before we saw him again.

When Carlos left, we never knew when he would come back. With him gone anywhere from six months to a year at times, my mother would work hard to create normalcy and move on with life. But he would always come back and force his way into our lives. It was a vicious cycle: drink – abuse – leave – return. He would show back up on the doorstep with an apology in tow. My mother would accept him back based on the fear that he would beat her or even kill her if she said no. But the eviction notice was the last straw for my mother. She had been working up the courage to leave Carlos for some time, and the eviction helped push her to make the final decision. My mother and sisters left Carlos on his knees in that alley and made their way toward our neighbor Eva's house.

Throughout the years, Eva and my mother had developed a strong friendship. We trusted her, and both women looked after one another. On the day of the eviction, Eva greeted my family with warmth and listened to my mother share her experience that morning. Eva grieved alongside her for the loss of our home and agreed to look after a few essential items and documents my mother needed to leave with her as she collected herself. My mother gave Eva legal paperwork about our home to safeguard.

Prior to our eviction, my mother met with a few lawyers in Los Angeles who did pro bono work in home ownership. She knew that we could no longer just wait for the new property owners to arrive and rent to our family. So, she decided to secretly fight to keep the house without the knowledge of my stepfather. My mother's willpower and determination to protect her family was the key to saving us from abuse and homelessness.

Who I Am

Champions are made from something they have deep inside them — a desire, a dream, a vision. They have to have the skill and the will. But the will must be stronger than the skill. — Muhammad Ali

At age sixteen, our eviction was a traumatic experience that caused me to look more closely at my life and family. Was I destined to follow in the cycle of poverty my mother had been born into? Or would my life be different?

Failure was a word I knew well. Not reaching one's potential was normal and almost an expectation within my neighborhood. Most of my peers accepted whatever cards they were dealt. Some followed a path of crime and joined gangs that eventually led to their death or incarceration. Others worked in back-breaking jobs just to earn minimum wage, never having the time or energy to dream about rising above the mediocre conditions around them.

Me during middle school at our home on Gramercy Place in South Los Angeles.

Like most things in my life, I tried to make sense of things through a sports analogy. I thought about the Phoenix Phenomenon — the rising of a new life from old remains. Sitting alone on my porch, surrounded by darkness, I knew in my heart I had to break free from generational hardship, let go of my old life, and rise from the ashes like a phoenix.

At the time, I did not realize the profound impact this one event would have on me. I now understand it to be my moment of transformation. It was the pivotal moment in my life where I was old enough to take control and create a different outcome for myself. I wanted to be better for my sisters and my mother. I wanted to be everything my stepfather and biological father could not be for us.

The thought of not having a place to live fired me up and pushed me to find my inner greatness over the next few years. I felt as if I had been lit on fire and became hyper-focused on finishing school and playing soccer. I prayed often and used the experience to fuel me.

I was ready to endure the hard road ahead and felt anointed by this journey. It was my time to rewrite my family's history and serve as a leader for our next generations. I rejected my hood's notion that I could only aspire for so much in life. God spoke to me and told me that I was about to embark on a journey through unknown territory— a journey that would change the trajectory of my family's lives forever.

Who I Come From

The women in my family have had the biggest influence on shaping the man I am today, especially my mother and my grandmother, *Abuela* Rosa Emília.

My grandmother Rosa Emília and my mother after my college graduation.

While my mother pushed me to be the best version of myself and provided for me, my grandmother was my best friend. I could listen to Abuela Rosa Emília tell stories for hours. She instilled a hard work ethic in my mother and taught her bravery in the most difficult of times. Abuela Rosa Emília guided my mother through some of the most challenging moments of her life and showed her how to stand up for herself, giving her the strength to immigrate to a distant foreign country.

My family's migration is like that of many of my peers. I grew up with dozens of kids from Central America, with similar backgrounds, whose parents had taken the same path to get to the United States. Like many of my friends, my family's story represents one of thousands of families' stories that go untold year after year.

As a journalist, I see and listen to these stories every day. Stories of immigrant caravans leaving Central America looking to escape violence and extreme poverty. Families, like mine, cross rivers, mountains, cities by bus, foot, and in the trunks of strange cars in search of a better life. The sacrifices my family made with their lives have given me and my sisters an ultimate gift. They have given me an opportunity to make something out of myself and accomplish things that had never been done before in our generational history.

From a young age, I had listened to my mother and grandmother's stories, but I never really understood what I was being told. Like so many other young Salvadoran children, I grew up listening to Abuela Rosa Emília telling folklore about Salvadoran mythical creatures like *La Siguanaba* — a Salvadoran tale similar to *La Llorona* — a woman ghost looking for children to kill. As I grew older and experienced my own challenges, I saw more of her stories beyond the fairytales. I gained a new perspective from her history. Listening to my grandmother speak about my family became an account of my own path. It was a blueprint for my foundation.

Abuela Rosa Emília and I during one of her birthdays. Abuela always saw her special day to reunite the entire family.

Every one of my family members had sacrificed something in order to give me a better life.

When they first came to the United States, my uncles and mother had a plan. They would work hard, save money and head back to El Salvador to buy a house for their family. They would be back home in just a few months, maybe years, but not too long. Little did my mother know she would stay in Los Angeles alongside her siblings to raise seven children of her own. She would endure life in a foreign country, where she did not speak the language, and would never return to her childhood home.

Their journey to the United States was a dream come true. A dream so big that hundreds of unaccompanied children embark on the journey alone to reach it. As a guest speaker at a middle school, I asked how many had come from Central America undocumented and alone. At just twelve years old, close to 90% of our group raised their hand. It was the first time I realized that

17

many of my peers had endured a similar experience to that of my mother, uncles, and grandmother. Central American families and children were making that same dangerous journey nearly forty years later. It made me feel distressed listening to them talk about the struggles and challenges they faced along the way. It also reinforced why I now have to share my family's and my personal story.

Where It All Started — El Salvador

I do not believe in death without resurrection. If they kill me, I will rise again in the people of El Salvador. — Oscar Romero

A land of volcanoes and beautiful beaches, El Salvador holds the foundation of our family roots.

My mother was born in San Miguel, a city within the department of San Miguel, which helped make up *El Oriente,* along with the departments of *Usúlutan, La Unión,* and *Morazán* in the eastern part of the country. Her home city borders Honduras to the north and the Pacific Ocean to the south. San Miguel also holds the *Chaparrastique* volcano, the most active of the twenty-three volcanoes throughout El Salvador. My mom used to tell us that she was born on top of that volcano.

Perhaps the easiest way to distinguish people from San Miguel is by the way they speak. People from the eastern city heavily use the letter "j" in their everyday vocabulary. For example, if you ask a person where they are from, they might answer "Jan Miguel" (han-Miguel) instead of pronouncing San Miguel.

This way of speaking can be attributed to the indigenous group, *Lencas,* that populated southwestern Honduras and El Oriente, the eastern part of El Salvador, before the Spanish invasion. The arrival of the Spanish forced the indigenous populations to adopt a new language foreign to their original form of communication, thus creating distinctions in speech like the use of "j."

The Lenca*s* only resided in the eastern part of El Salvador, while most of the country was inhabited by the indigenous people that spoke *Nahua Pipil.* This explains the distinctions in accents. This notable difference in expression is one that people outside of San Miguel tended to look down upon and refer to as poor usage of the Spanish language.

Despite the cultural variation and bias within my mother's home country of El Salvador, it is important to note that the Lenca language is now almost extinct. The unique pieces of my family's

19

history are a legacy that gave my mother, aunts, and uncles tenacity; a determination that I would like to believe was passed on to me.

El Salvador is the smallest and most populated of the seven nations that make up Central America. Historically, El Salvador has wrestled with high levels of poverty and very little educational attainment. This has pushed the majority of the population into low-paying, manual labor-type jobs that don't require a certification, such as the cultivation of coffee, cotton, corn, and sugarcane.

The people of El Salvador can be described as humble and hardworking, willing to do whatever it takes to earn *el pan de cada día* — daily bread — a phrase used in many Salvadoran households. Much of the population faces hard work daily, which in most cases doesn't allow for much academic or professional growth.

San Miguel is the most important commercial center of eastern El Salvador, producing textiles, rope, leather goods, fruit, basic grains, and oleaginous seeds. The region provided opportunities yet going to school was a privilege only the rich could afford. Education was never a real option for my grandparents; therefore, it was never prioritized in their home. This meant my mother and her siblings started working from a very young age.

My mother started helping my abuela — grandmother — Rosa Emília with work around the same age my grandmother had helped her own father. Around the age of six, my mother was already my grandmother's *mano derecha* — right hand, the person you most trust and can depend on — a phrase my grandmother repeated when remembering my mother as a child.

As a young girl, when she wasn't out in the town selling food, my mother was home taking care of her siblings. One day when my mother was around ten years old, my abuela headed out to sell *chicharrones* — fried pork — and other Salvadoran appetizers while my mom stayed behind at a family member's house. It was rare that she didn't accompany her mother, but on this day, my mother decided to take the opportunity to spend time with her own grandmother, who usually asked for help when she came over to her house.

That day, my grandmother Rosa Emília gave clear directions to my mother not to leave the house for any reason, including any errands. A few hours after Abuela Rosa Emília left, my mother's aunt asked her to make herself useful and work. In her attempt to be obedient, my mom followed directions and headed to the local *molino* — corn mill — to grind corn. The molino used industrial, electric grinders to make *la masa* — cornmeal — for handmade tortillas, among other things.

My mother left her grandmother's home carrying a basket full of corn to the mill, which was managed by another child around her age. Upon arrival, she wasted little time and began depositing all the corn she had brought into the grinders. The machines were churning with their metal gears, moiling kernels into a smooth dust, when the facility lost electricity and the equipment abruptly halted.

My mother's first reaction was to recover everything left inside the grinder. In order to do that, she needed to take it out by hand. She didn't want to be scolded for losing the corn she had been given by her aunt to grind. With her hands still inside the machine, power at the mill was restored and gears began to turn again. My mother screamed for help, and the near adolescent manager ran to shut everything back down.

My mother winced, attempting to remove her hand, but her fingers were stuck behind the metal plates inside the machinery. While the young plant manager called for help, my mother lost consciousness and fainted.

Meanwhile, my grandmother was selling popular snacks outside the Francisco Barraza stadium where San Miguel's professional soccer team, *Águila*, played. The stadium was roaring with loud cheers like it usually did for the team's games when rumors of a tragedy unfolding at the local corn mill caught Abuela Rosa Emília's attention.

A girl was mentioned to be at the center of the terrible scene described, and my grandmother interrupted the recounting of graphic details to inquire about the girl's physical description. With only a brief reply of "she has curly hair," Abuela Rosa Emília dropped her business and ran. Each of the individually packaged treats she had worked so hard to prepare fell to the ground as she raced home.

When she arrived at the molino, police officers would not allow her inside and instead gave her the painful details that my mother was unconscious, still stuck inside the machine. Hours had passed at this point because the owner would not allow the paramedics to disassemble his equipment. Instead, the owner suggested that they cut my mother's hand off to break her free.

It wasn't until my great-grandfather — my *bisabuelo* — Concepción arrived with a machete in his belt and rifle in hand that everyone on the scene paid attention to my grandmother's need to be with her daughter. In front of the police, Bisabuelo Concepción pointed the gun at the owner's head and told him that if he didn't break the grinder apart, he would blow his head clean off. Concepción was a respected man around town, and he always showed up to defend his family. The owner conceded.

Not long after the showdown, the authorities dismantled the machinery to liberate my mother's hand. Her fingers had been crushed and were deemed useless by doctors at the local hospital. Although only the three middle fingers of her right hand were no longer salvageable, the medical crew attempted to amputate almost her entire hand. After negotiations with my Abuela Rosa Emília, the doctors agreed to only remove the affected fingers. My mother's thumb and pinky finger were saved.

While that day at the mill haunted my grandmother with a pain she carried until her death, it seemed to make my mother stronger. My mother's mangled hand caused her to be ridiculed by school friends and even family members throughout her childhood. However, if she was ever hurt or embarrassed, she never showed it. The traumatizing experience forced my mother to develop thicker skin and to ignore what people said about her.

Losing three fingers at such a young age demanded that my mother learn new ways of doing things. She had to re-learn basic, everyday tasks such as eating and picking up different items. Simple things were challenging and often uncomfortable, as people constantly stared and whispered while pointing at her.

My mother always told me that overcoming such an injury and the embarrassment that followed made her feel like she could accomplish anything. This self-confidence, bravery, and grit are what would eventually allow my mother to embark on the dangerous and daunting trek from El Salvador to the United States, a 3,000-mile journey on bus, train, and foot.

Digging Deeper

We are not makers of history. We are made by history. — Martin Luther King

When the Spaniards left Central America in the 1800s, all of El Salvador's power and resources were transferred to those of European ancestry. Wealth and control were designated to *las catorce familias* — the fourteen families — who would rule the country for decades. The rest of the population, made up of indigenous peoples and *mestizos* — individuals of mixed European and indigenous ancestry — were left to survive in what would become something of a feudal society.

With the turn of the 20th century, coffee became the economic driver for El Salvador and the fourteen families dominated the industry. The families selected presidents among themselves and ruled through a military dictatorship. The aristocracy also supported laws that prevented workers from moving, thus controlling much of their lives.

In 1929, the stock market crash halted the coffee-driven economy. The poor were forced out of work by the *las catorce familias*, causing the indigenous and peasant populations to organize against the elite. In 1932, Agustín Farabundo Martí led an uprising against the ruling dictatorship. The rebellion was crushed within days and over 30,000 people were killed; almost all of them were indigenous and poor Salvadorans. This massacre was known as *La Matanza*.

My great-grandmother Transito Vásquez, known as Mama Tanchito, was just a little girl during La Matanza but shared vivid memories of the events that took place. The news of indigenous murder was rampant throughout El Salvador, and our family was terrified for many years that they might also be killed due to our strong indigenous lineage. Unfortunately, this would not be the last time my family's country experienced such horrific levels of violence.

24

After La Matanza, El Salvador and the families living there, including my own, endured years of harsh authoritarian control. However, the massacre did not extinguish the desire for reform for the nation's poor and is widely considered the precursor to the violent civil war that would plague the population.

In 1972, co-founder of the new Christian Democrat Party (PDC) José Duarte ran for president. Despite receiving the majority vote, the presidency was appointed to his opponent in what is considered a fraudulent election. Soon after, a coup attempted by leftist military supporters left Duarte exiled and his followers murdered by the government-supported death squads.

Political unrest continued to grow throughout the 1970s under the militant control of the National Conciliation Party (PCN). In 1979, the *Junta Revolucionaria de Gobierno* (JRG), a left-wing combined civilian and military government, deposed President Carlos Humberto Romero and assumed power. With the encouragement of the JRG, Duarte returned to El Salvador in 1980 to join the junta as they attempted to address the country's poverty and disparities, later acting as president. While promising democratization and reform, the JRG was still a military dictatorship that resulted in a surge of right-wing violence.

With the coup came war, and the JRG struggled to maintain control. Their most prolific right-wing opponent arose in Salvadoran army officer, Roberto D'Aubuisson, also known as "Blowtorch Bob." He founded the Nationalist Republican Alliance party (ARENA) and remained a central leader of the death squads throughout the war. D'Aubuisson was suspected of having orchestrated the assassination of San Salvador's Archbishop Oscar Romero in March of 1980. An event that plunged the country into full-blown civil war after thousands of mourners were gunned down at his funeral. With all sides utilizing death squads and guerilla warfare, the civilian population cowered under the violent threat of bombings, shootings, kidnaps, and murders.

Decades later, my family still remembers the war as if it were yesterday. Of those that had lived in El Salvador during this time, almost all confirmed that they had almost encountered death at least once. Even my hyper-masculine, *macho* uncles have had to pause and quickly recover from the pain they feel when remembering triggering moments from that time.

Tío Oscar — Uncle Oscar — was a musician and moved around the country a lot as a teenager. His craft allowed him to see parts of El Salvador that many of my other relatives weren't able to enjoy. His traveling also exposed him to new forms of violence that exploded throughout the country during the late 1970s and early 1980s. On more than one occasion, Tío Oscar recalled the memories of seeing bodies hanging from trees, fences, or light posts. Such public displays of death were, unfortunately, very common.

My uncle Robert served as part of the military, and his position saved several family members during that time on more than one occasion. Like hundreds of others, Tío Robert joined the military at the age of sixteen and was forced to fight during the civil war. He has always sworn that he never killed an innocent person and only shot a weapon against guerrillas in his time as a soldier. He often told a story of a mission his brigade had been assigned. A guerilla location in the forest had been discovered. They were sent to shut it down or "eliminate the threat." Tío Robert recalls that this really meant that they were to kill everyone in the camp. As they went deeper into the forest, he remembered that something didn't feel right about the mission, and about an hour into the jungle, they were ambushed by guerrilla fighters. They had fallen into a trap and were attacked from every angle.

My uncle doesn't remember how he made it out of the forest alive, but he does recount that there were only two survivors that day, and he was one of them. He often told us that death was always lurking around them. Every day soldiers put on their uniforms knowing that it could be their last.

My abuela had a gambling addiction when she was younger to help her cope with the abuse she suffered at the hands of my grandfather, Luis Moreno. She often spent her evenings playing cards with local neighbors late into the hours of the night. As the war escalated, curfews were implemented to prevent soldiers from mistaking civilians for guerrilla fighters. One cold night, my grandmother left a poker game wearing a scarf to cover her face to shield her from the wind. Her scarf was red, the color worn by the leftist guerrilla forces — the Farabundo Martí National Liberation Front (FMLN) — and could be spotted from a mile away. Minutes after leaving for her place, a military jeep spotted her and turned the lights on in her direction, causing her to freeze. She heard ¡alto! — stop — and a soldier got out of the truck, walking towards her with his gun pointed in her direction.

The soldier questioned my grandmother at gunpoint about where she was coming from at this time of night. Embarrassed, my grandmother refused to admit she had been gambling and would not answer the soldier's questions. With the rifle pointed at her head, she knew that she was one step away from being shot and killed.

In a moment of desperation, Abuela Rosa Emília mentioned my Tio Robert and his position in the military. The soldiers, now three of them standing around my grandmother, pulled her back to the truck by her hair and slapped her around a few times before driving toward her home. She was released that night with a warning that if she was lying about my Tio Robert or caught breaking curfew again, she would not be so lucky the next time.

All It Takes Is One

All it takes is one drop to start a ripple effect. — Austin Gregg

Seeking to flee the death and violence of El Salvador, many of my family members decided *nos vamos para el norte* — we will head to the north. People were fleeing by the thousands. Some were fortunate enough to obtain political asylum, allowing for an easier and legal entry into the U.S. Others, in fear for their lives and unable to wait for the asylum process, would embark on a journey to the U.S. through Guatemala and México.

Tio Oscar was the first to leave. Only a teenager at the time, he decided to travel with a group of friends who were heading north. He was swayed by common Central American stories that dollar bills fell from trees in the United States and that all you had to do was pick the money up off the ground. Oscar's group was led by a man named Marcos Cornejo, who was running away from the military that had murdered his entire family for failing to pay a randomly imposed bi-weekly fee. After months of extortion, Marcos was determined to leave the country immediately, and his conviction led to many others in the neighborhood agreeing to go with him.

Tio Oscar left with the group, only making it as far as México's capital city, *Ciudad de México,* where he lived for seven months. While in México, Oscar worked on the rails of the city's subway, a job he found after meeting a few locals who enjoyed his outgoing personality accompanied by an eccentric look and a wild afro.

Weeks after his arrival in México City, Tio Oscar finally notified my family in San Miguel. His departure inspired his sister Miriam — my *tia* or aunt — to embark on her own journey north. When Miriam made her way toward the United States, she stopped in México City. Using the address from his original letter, she managed to track down my uncle after a few days. She showed up at his job unexpectedly, and their reunion prompted them to progress further ahead to Los Angeles.

However, neither Tio Oscar nor my Tia Miriam could find peace in their new location. They were unable to stop thinking of their family back in El Salvador, where the violence raged on. It was decided that Tio Oscar would go back to San Miguel to bring the whole family north, where they could all be together.

As a U.S. citizen, I grew up hearing my mother, aunts, uncles, and grandmother tell me how fortunate my siblings and I were for being born in the U.S. We could do things that people who came to the country undocumented could not. We had basic rights like the ability to speak up against injustice without the fear of being deported. These were rights and privileges that my siblings and I would sometimes take for granted. Rights that millions who come to the United States pray that they can one day obtain.

The great Salvadoran *diaspora* of the 1980s led my family to the city of Los Angeles like thousands of others fleeing a twelve-year, brutal civil war that killed more than 75,000 people by the end of the conflict in 1992. According to my mother and uncles, leaving El Salvador was never an easy choice for my family, but it was a sacrifice that had to be made in order to have a better life and chase the "American Dream." Tio Oscar and Tia Miriam's experiences became a large part of my family's decision to risk everything in search of opportunity in California. My mother was twenty years old the day she left for the U.S.

Heading North

You don't know how strong you are until being strong is your only choice.
— Bob Marley

In October 1982, at 5:00am, my mother gathered a few of her personal belongings to set out on the long, harsh migration to the United States. It was just a year after the massacre of "El Mozote" where an entire mountain village of almost one thousand people were murdered by the military. There was only one survivor. The massacre occurred less than two hours away from their city. My family was finally ready to head north. They were choosing to fight for their right to live by leaving their native country.

With Tio Oscar guiding my mother, Tio Robert, and my two cousins, they first had to cross almost the entire country of El Salvador by bus to the border with Guatemala. For my mother, this initial leg of the trip promised both unknown excitement and some anxiety. She had only ever been as far as San Salvador when traveling outside of her city. It wasn't until she turned around to look back at her childhood home one more time that a river of emotions washed over her body. Gazing back at the mountain-filled skyline, she realized that she was leaving the only home she had ever known, and there was no certainty that she would ever return. With every step forward, she was one step further away from the land that birthed her, her beautiful country that was now tearing itself apart.

The trip promised to be especially challenging, as my aunt Miriam's young sons Ernesto and Gilberto were joining at just five and four-years-old. As the only female of the group, my mother was responsible for them. This occupied more of her focus as she grieved from leaving her mother and country behind.

In control of their course, Tio Oscar guided my family toward their first stop in *Guate* — a common term for Guatemala — where they stayed for a night before getting back on the road toward México. The journey from San Miguel to Guatemala

City was around seventeen hours, with one stop in San Salvador. In San Salvador, my family would transfer buses for the first of many times on this venture. They reached Ciudad Tecún Umán — a border city with Ciudad Hidalgo, México — in just a few days. Despite Tio Oscar's concerns about traveling with small children, they made excellent time into México. Tecún Umán is a common stop that thousands of Central American immigrants cross every day to get closer to *el norte* — the north. Whether migrants have legal documentation or not, hundreds of thousands just like my family cross the Suchiate River in search of a better life in the United States.

When my mother speaks about her journey to the U.S., she stops to take a deep breath as she remembers some of the bad things they went through. Crossing the border from Guatemala into México was supposed to be simple. Lack of money forced them into situations where they had to risk their lives. Instead of paying to bribe authorities in México, they had to cross the Suchiate River, where they would spend another night before they kept moving. Tio Oscar believed the river would be chest-deep at its deepest point, estimating the greatest depth to be approximately four feet. My mother couldn't swim; exacerbated by her being barely five feet tall and carrying a child on her back, the situation quickly turned into a life-threatening mistake.

After only a short distance into the river, my mother slipped on the loose sand beneath her. With my four-year-old cousin still holding onto her, she struggled to get afloat. With Gilberto gripping onto her tightly, my mother screamed *ayuda* — help — fighting to keep them both above the surface. Gilberto's tiny voice shouted "Tia!" just as Tio Robert grabbed my mother's thick, curly hair, the last visible part of her to pull her back to safety. With everyone safely back on the shore, my uncles re-strategized the group's path. Deciding to bring the two young boys across the river first and going back to help my mother cross safely.

My mother recalls the experience as one that both terrified and prepared her for what was yet to come. The fear of almost drowning raised doubts in her about her decision to leave El Salvador. However, she also remembers feeling the presence of

31

God and understanding that He was revealing her strength as a sign that she would need to have persistent faith to survive the rest of their journey.

After getting across the Suchiate River, my family took a bus to Tapachula to eat before continuing on. This was their first meal in México, and the first time they had eaten since leaving Guatemala. Stopping at a taco vendor to taste authentic tacos for the first time, my mother was asked whether she wanted her tacos *caliente o frio* — hot or cold. Unfamiliar with Mexican customs and phrases of speech, my mother thought the vendor was asking about the temperature of her food and naturally replied that she wanted her tacos hot. Caliente also means spicy and, unfortunately for my mother, she had actually selected the spicy option. With her tongue pulsing from the heat after one bite, my mother realized just how far away she was from the *pupusas* and *panes con pollo* of San Miguel.

My mother was forced to finish her mouth-numbing tacos, as the timing of their next meal was unknown and heavily dependent on financial help provided by my Tia Miriam in the U.S. Between three adults and two children, the money sent was just enough to pay for transportation to the next stop, where they would check in with Tia Miriam and wait for additional funds to be sent. With little left over to feed and shelter them, much of my family's travel through México was supported by the kindness of the Mexican people. Walking north from town to town, my family asked strangers for places to stay for a night and rides to move them closer to Los Angeles.

It took my family over a month just to travel the 126 miles from Ciudad Hidalgo to México's capital — *Ciudad de Mexico.* This was the sometimes overwhelming city my Tio Oscar had called home for almost a year prior to this journey. They arrived at a bus terminal about an hour away from their destination and decided to walk the rest of the way to avoid any additional risk. My mother's strong Salvadoran accent was deemed too noticeable by my uncles, and they instructed her not to speak under any circumstances.

As they walked along bustling streets, with the smell of delicious *tacos*, *gorditas*, and *sopes* filling their noses, their empty bellies yearned for something to eat. They walked miles across the city with hunger pains. Focused on their destination, they finally arrived at La Colonia Atlacomulco, a small area outside the capital city, where a man named Andrés García would let them stay for a few nights.

During Tio Oscar's time in México City, he and Andrés had worked together on the train rails and had become good friends. Andrés was a good man with a big heart. His mantra was *tu familia es mi familia* — your family is my family. My family would stay with Andrés' family for almost two months as they waited for my aunt Miriam to send more money.

At the García home in Colonia Atlacomulco, none of my five family members ever went hungry, eating three meals almost every day. Andrés' hospitality and stability also proved to be important for Ernesto and Gilberto. Being so young, the journey was especially tough on them, and the almost two-month period of security gave the boys peace in a time of great uncertainty.

My mother, on the other hand, remembers her impatience during this portion of the trip. She wasn't allowed to venture outside Andrés' home and felt stuck inside a room babysitting the young boys. My uncles would leave her alone for hours, escaping the pressures and difficulty of the trip, a privilege their male gender allowed them in "machismo" culture.

Tia Miriam's money from the north eventually arrived, and my uncles and mother were forced to say goodbye to a new family that they would likely never see again. The García family refused compensation for their hospitality and, instead, only asked that my family never forget their time together. This was a promise my family has always upheld. I can't recall one story in which the García family wasn't mentioned in the story of our journey north.

From Colonia Atlacomulco, my family would take a bus approximately six hours to the city of Guadalajara in the state of Jalisco, México, the halfway point from El Salvador to Los

Angeles. Upon arrival, they would only exit the bus for a few hours before they reboarded again for the next leg of the expedition. Like many of the stops before, Guadalajara was only a place to change buses while allowing them to quickly stretch and buy a cheap meal.

In total, the bus ride from México City to Tijuana, México, with one stop in Guadalajara, took almost forty hours and covered more than 1,400 miles. By bus, my family would pass through Tepic, the capital of Nayarit, a state in the western part of México, known for its colorful, colonial buildings set in the middle of hills near the Sanganguey volcano. They drove through cities in Sinaloa like Mazatlán, a coastal town, now known as a popular resort town with access to the Pacific Ocean and French Baroque influences in its historic downtown area. And Culiacán, Sinaloa's largest city, permeated by the Humaya and Tamazula and Culiacán that gave life to tranquil, lush gardens.

As the hours passed and they watched colorful colonial buildings leave their views from the bus windows, my family began to imagine what their life might be like when they finally made it to L.A. Their fantasies only became more real as they approached Tijuana. Almost two days after leaving the Mexican capital, the group descended the bus in La Terminal de Tecate about an hour and a half from Tijuana. Drained of energy and agitated, my family was near a breaking point. Hunger and fatigue overwhelmed everyone, including the usually lively young boys.

Nevertheless, my family was now so close to the border that they could smell the freedom the United States promised just a few miles away. The "American Dream" was just a short distance from where they stood.

My family had just finalized a trip through three countries, with very little to eat and in fear for their safety much of the time. It was a trip that had taken a lot from all of them — mentally, emotionally, and physically.

The American Dream Just Feet Away

My family had come so far, yet the next leg of their trip to Los Angeles would be the hardest part yet. My Tio Oscar's guidance would come to an end in Tijuana. He decided he wasn't capable enough to overcome the last hurdle. The thought of failing and being sent back to El Salvador with four other people pushed him to hire a *coyote* — a human smuggler. He had served as a coyote from San Miguel to the border with the U.S, but that's as far as he would go under that role. He wasn't as familiar with the border and didn't know what specific spots to use in order to cross into San Diego. Coyotes, on the other hand, studied the border and knew exactly when to make a move.

Crossing the U.S. border was difficult, and they would need the perfect coyote to get them to the other side. Coyotes make a living based on crossing people into the United States. A billion-dollar underground industry built on trust and word of mouth. Hiring the right person for the job is one of the most important things during this trek. Stories of people being charged thousands of dollars and left stranded traveled all the way back to El Salvador. In some instances, people would be handed over to gangs who would extort them for whatever money they had.

Smugglers could best be defined as ruthless and willing to do whatever it took to get paid, even if it meant screwing people over. Unlike other people before, there were no recommendations for any particular coyote. Instead, they would have to look for one based on their gut feeling.

As they waited for the last of Tia Miriam's money to come, they rented a small room in Tijuana, determining their next steps. In the early 1980s, the price for getting across the border was around $400 USD per adult and almost $200 USD per child. They found a room in an area of Tijuana called Colonia Madero, also known as Cacho, which became their home for a week while Tia Miriam pulled together the hefty sum for their crossing.

The front desk operator assumed my family was like so many other families he had seen passing through his city and inquired about their need for a coyote. He got them in contact with a coyote he knew from the area. Fear ran through my mother's mind as she wondered if the coyote would attempt to rape her or leave her in the middle of nowhere. He seemed so confident that he would get all three members of my family across safely that my uncles felt relieved and grateful that they had been so fortunate to have encountered the man at the front desk of their hotel. Little did they know that this reassurance was something that, in the best-case scenario, the coyote had very little control over.

As they spoke over the phone about how they would be crossing the border, the smugglers had a different plan for Gilberto and Ernesto. The boys would cross by car, unnoticed, through the busy border crossing that connected Tijuana and San Diego. They would be dressed up like little girls to get past immigration officers with fake documents. To get to the other side without the boys crying or asking questions, both Ernesto and Gilberto would be sedated to appear as if they were waking up from a nap. They would then be driven directly to Los Angeles, where their mother waited for them.

The coyote's plan seemed so simple and, for the first time ever, my family could see their future just ahead in the city of San Diego. Lights radiated from the U.S. city as if to confirm that all of their aspirations were alive just a few feet away. As they stood on the Mexican side of the border, my family breathed a sigh of relief. They were closer to their freedom.

On the day of their crossing, my mother's heart pounded in her chest as if it was trying to escape her ribcage. One minor mistake would be enough to earn them a ticket back to the violence and poverty they left behind in El Salvador. She thought back to all they had been through. She had almost drowned in Guatemala just a couple of months before and recalled her seemingly petty frustration at being half stuck in a room in Atlacomulco. It was unbelievable how far she had come; the journey was almost complete. That evening, as the sun began to set, my mother got down on her knees and prayed for God to help them overcome one last hurdle safely into the United States.

In front of their small hotel, they met the coyote who would be leading them into San Diego. He was ghastly thin, around seventy years old, with only one eye. My uncles and mother looked in shock at one another. This could not have been the man they spoke to on the phone. But they swallowed their fear and decided to trust the one-eyed smuggler. He at least worked with the confident man they had spoken to on the phone and likely knew how to get them across as well. They had also paid their money and were not in any position to argue otherwise.

After only a few minutes, the adults stopped in front of the U.S. Mexican border, the entry point into San Diego they would attempt crossing. The darkness surrounded them and prevented anyone from seeing anything more than five feet away. My mother could hear the sirens of patrol cars nearby and the violent flapping of helicopter propellers above them. The one-eyed coyote repeated over and over for them not to worry. He explained that the helicopters flying over the area and the blaring police sirens were normal sounds around the border.

By direction of the smuggler, they hid in the bushes as a helicopter soared straight over them. He seemed tense and a little concerned, but shook it off and instructed them to continue walking forward toward the lights at the border. Within minutes, several border patrol vehicles pulled up to block their path forward. Red and blue lights surrounded them, and sirens blared so loudly that they froze in place. Officers yelled for them to keep still or it would cost them their lives. Everyone stopped as officers yelled at them to lie on the ground with their arms and legs spread. Their hands were then tied with zip ties before being placed inside a vehicle to transport them back to the station.

It was over. Their first attempt to enter the United States had ended in failure. They were instructed not to reveal who was leading the group once taken into custody. Detained, my mother and uncles devised a plan to avoid being deported all the way back to El Salvador. They would say they were from México to be released at the border. This was a fabrication that proved to be much more difficult for my mother, who had been separated from my uncles and placed in a room with another woman for questioning.

Before the officers entered for questioning, my mother asked the woman where she was from in preparation for the lie she was about to tell. The woman was Mexican and understood my mother's frantic attempt to save herself from deportation. Together they went over as many common cultural details as possible, from the history of the Mexican flag to the national anthem. My family had been warned that the border patrol would often ask common cultural questions about México in an effort to determine whether or not a person was really Mexican. A wrong answer would almost certainly send you with a one-way ticket back to Central America, while answering correctly might mean you were released in Tijuana.

When the officers finally entered the room, their first question was to ask where my mother was from. She responded that she was from México in a forced push to hide her Salvadoran accent. The officers weren't convinced. They asked her to name the colors of the Mexican flag. Flustered, she responded with green and white, omitting the color red in her stressed state. The immigration officers insisted she was from Central America, despite her appeals to maintain her false Mexican identity.

Unaware that she was being watched from a distance, my mother fought to hold back tears, certain that the end was near. With a knock at the window of the interrogation room, a supervisor motioned for the officers to bring her into his office to speak with her. When my mother made it to the supervisor's office, she couldn't help but feel uncomfortable by the way the man was staring at her. He had a profound look, and his gaze seemed to follow her every movement as she entered the office to sit before his desk. His intensity confused my mother, making her feel even more uncertain of her fate and what would come to her next.

An Unexpected Offer

The supervisor spoke. In a gentle form, he asked her to tell him the truth about her origins because he was there to help her. Unsurprised by my mother's hesitant silence to break away from the lie she had just told the other officers, the supervisor continued to speak in an effort to gain my mother's trust. He went on to say that he had a daughter around her age that he loved very much who had passed away. That daughter reminded him of my mother and compelled him to help her in any way that he was able.

Disconcerted and unsure of what to say, my mother broke down and finally told the man the truth about where she was from. Honesty took over, and she confessed that she had traveled all the way from El Salvador to escape the violence that threatened her life almost every day. My mother told the supervisor how she had just recently been held at gunpoint. She told him that she needed to flee in order to survive. The truth poured out of her in a way that surprised her, not realizing the emotional toll the civil war had taken upon her emotions and her body. It felt as if God was speaking through her. She was healing and regaining her strength. Despite her authenticity with the immigration commander, she maintained that she was traveling alone. She knew that the kindness bestowed upon her as a young woman that resembled a man's daughter would likely not extend to her brothers. The last thing she wanted was to jeopardize the safety of Oscar and Robert.

The supervisor listened to my mother's story intently and without interruption. When she had finished, the man paused and, with a deep breath, offered to help her if she stayed in México near him. He asked her not to move forward with her plans to cross over into the U.S. He told her that if she stayed in Tijuana, he would help her finish school. While she studied, she could stay with family friends of his.

My mother was stunned. The supervisor's kindness and genuine gesture to support her through school were overwhelming for her, especially in her vulnerable state. As appealing as the opportunity sounded, she felt the tug in her chest toward Los Angeles. Staying in México wasn't a part of her plan. School in Tijuana did not even feel like a real option. She wanted to finish the trip north and reunite with her family members in California. With the courage that had pulled honesty from her, she politely declined the man's offer. She told him that she had obligations to reunite and provide for her family in both El Salvador and the U.S.

In what she felt was a divine intervention, my mother was released from the detention center without a record of her even being held. No fingerprints nor any information about her undocumented crossing was taken down. Almost a million and a half people per year were attempting to reach the United States during the 1980s, 1990s, and well into the next decade, just like my mother and uncles. My mother's experience was one that almost no other person was afforded when being detained for crossing the border into the U.S. without the proper documentation. Decades later, immigrants who sought to come into the country only had to make it to the border and turn themselves in, asking for asylum.

My mother's good fortune did not end with her release. The supervisor paid for her taxi back to the small hotel. He also gave her a little extra cash to buy some food. Escorting my mother to the front of the station, the supervisor requested that the officers make sure my mother was fed and safely returned back to the place she was staying. Both of my uncles were eventually released but, unlike my mother, their fingerprints and information had been collected by immigration.

Get Up and Try Again

Back together in the Tijuana hotel, my family learned that the boys, Ernesto and Gilberto, had made it safely to Los Angeles. This eased some of their anxiety. Now they could start planning again, this time with a different coyote.

My uncles ventured into the downtown area to begin scouting their luck at local markets, restaurants, and bars. It didn't take them long to find a few locals in town that were connected to a few smugglers able to take them across the border. The coyote business was a lucrative one in a border city like Tijuana.

My family's second attempt to cross would be led by a group of smugglers. This time, they would be guided by so-called "gangster coyotes." Their clothing and slang words quickly put the three adults on notice. It wasn't long before they began talking about how they controlled the streets of Tijuana. Elaborating about their multiple underground businesses, my uncles assumed were the selling of drugs. These men had a terrifying presence about them. They were bigger and stronger than the one-eyed, skeletal-looking man that had led them up to the border before. While my family felt anxious in their silent transactions with the gangsters, they believed the town consensus that these men were experts in border crossings. My uncles had received their names from several people in the bustling city center of Tijuana.

After sharing their failed attempt with the front desk staff at the hotel, this approach came highly recommended by the man working upfront. The gentleman had been disappointed that his previous referral had caused my family so much anguish, and he affirmed that he thought this next time, with more coyotes, they would make it across. As a gesture of apology and kindness, the hotel attendant gave them a free meal which they eagerly accepted. Money was tight, especially as they needed additional funds to pay the new group of coyotes to bring them into San Diego.

My family had arranged a payment plan with the coyotes this time. Tia Miriam was not able to send the large sum of money required for all three members to cross at once and the hotel costs were counterproductive to them coming up with the total funds needed for the crossing. My family understood that another failure to cross was not an option. It could mean that they were stuck in México for an indefinite amount of time.

Two days passed from their initial deposit with the band of mobster-like coyotes, and the time had come for my mother and uncles to cross again. They would travel again by night and left the hotel to meet the two men at 9:00pm. My family joined the coyotes and a larger group of about nine migrants from México and Central America, also hopeful for entry into the United States. The group approached another entrance point along the border from the area my family had made their first attempt, only a few days prior.

A total of a dozen migrants was led by two coyotes who didn't talk much, only warning them not to fall behind. The rest of the group was made up of two men, three women from México, a pair from Guatemala, and the rest were unknown because they didn't say a word during the crossing. Everyone had a look of concern as they walked along the border, afraid of being caught by border patrol. Some of the men traveling whispered among themselves about their families that were waiting for their arrival in different parts of Southern California. Two of the women were older than my mother and talked in very low voices about the fear of their loved ones not being able to pay the fees. Everyone had different concerns but shared the same goal of making it to the other side.

The new site seemed to have more people traveling by foot around the border and less air and patrol vehicle traffic. The dirt road was dark and only lit by the flashlights of the coyotes leading their way forward. The path was littered with rocks and dips, causing them to stumble from time to time as they worked to keep up with the rapid pace set by the men. My mother was walking alongside another woman who was around twenty-four years old, crossing for a second time after being deported from the U.S. She traveled alone in the hopes of making it back to her family. Falling out of the flashlight's range of illumination, the woman tripped and fell into a ditch about 150 meters deep, pulling my mother down into the hole with her as she attempted to break her fall.

My mother felt the absence of the woman's body that had been closely moving with her in the dimly lit trail. She and the woman were gripped with panic and called out to the coyotes to stop and save them. The women had managed to break her fall by hanging onto branches of the desert bushes that covered much of the perimeter of their path. The smugglers slowed down and argued amongst themselves about whether or not to rescue the women or leave them behind. Border crossing is an event of speed. The coyotes knew that they only had seconds to move the group from one point to the next before border patrol could appear and take them all into custody. Falling behind was bad for business.

As the group pleaded for the coyotes to slow down, a few men in the group, along with my uncles, quickly organized themselves to drop down and pull both women out of the pit. They all understood the importance of time, and they acted swiftly enough to save my mother and the other woman and rushed to get the group back in pace with the smugglers and their flashlights. It was another win over death for everyone.

The group concentrated on the ground ahead of them and walked for hours in silence through the dark. The woman's fall and the threat of being abandoned in the desert at night left a somber mood over everyone so that they could only focus on putting one foot in front of the other. Then, the coyotes casually mentioned that they were all on American soil. My family had finally made it to San Diego. They had been successful in getting across the border. The excitement for their future in the United States brought about new energy that melted my family's feelings of exhaustion away.

Their jubilation at achieving what had seemed impossible just days prior, however, was short-lived with the realization that their journey was hardly over. Crossing the border didn't mean my family was safe, nor did it mean their travel was complete. My uncles and mother would still need to travel another 120 miles to Los Angeles in a foreign land, without the proper documentation to move safely.

The sun began to rise, and the coyotes led the group to a thick cluster of bushes on a hill. My family would hide on that hill in San Diego for almost an entire day. My uncles and mother waited under the inconsistent shade of the bushes, without food and very little water, until a van arrived to take everyone to their next destination. It was nearly nightfall again. My uncles and mother piled into the van behind two men that were traveling north alone to find work and send money back to their families in México. The twelve migrants and two lead coyotes made their way to a safe house in San Diego under the dimly lit sky of sunset shifting into evening.

The house in San Diego had two bedrooms with simply made-up beds and thin mats and blankets for more migrants to rest on floors. Women and children huddled in corners to rest together under a roof after eating their small portions of eggs and beans with a piece of bread provided by an older Mexican lady that was working in the coyote's home.

Their arrival in San Diego made my mother very happy. In the safe house, she felt more at peace than she had in months. Looking around at the men, women, and children crowded in the modest home, she also wondered about the lives they had left behind. It broke her heart to witness the number of people fleeing their homes just like her. Many of the families were from Central America, and she wondered how many of them had feared for their safety. How many of them had come from extreme poverty? She knew it wasn't easy to leave family and memories behind for the unknown. In that safe house, my mother reflected on how grateful she felt to be alive after she had encountered so much death and pain.

My uncles and mother willingly took their plates and washed down their first hot meal in almost two days with a glass of room temperature water. They found a mat for my mother to lie on in the living room while my uncles sat near her with their backs against a wall as they waited for the final part of the journey. The following morning, they would travel by car to Los Angeles.

The next morning my uncles connected with Tia Miriam to prepare the money for their final payment for the crossing. Without any more money of her own, my aunt borrowed the last installment to the coyotes from friends in her neighborhood. Coyotes never allowed families to leave unless they were paid in full or had some type of sure-fire payment plan. My uncles wanted to get to Los Angeles to be with their sister and start working to repay the loans Tia Miriam took out for their travel and to send money back to my grandmother in San Miguel. Time was important.

A vehicle long in length, similar to a Chrysler Imperial from the '70s, arrived at the safe house that afternoon to take my two uncles, mother, and five other migrants from the San Diego house to Los Angeles. Tio Robert and Tio Oscar, along with another man, were placed in the trunk with a few small holes added for air. My mother and another woman were strategically placed on the floor between the front and the back seat. Two other men traveling sat in the back as normal passengers traveling from San Diego to Los Angeles. One of the coyotes drove and his companion rode in the passenger seat with a woman in between his legs. The vehicle was over capacity but, to the naked eye, it appeared to be a normal drive.

No one spoke during the almost five-hour trip to Los Angeles. Typically, the drive would take only about two and a half hours, but their trip doubled with a number of stops along the way to avoid being caught by the police or stopped at the final border patrol station. About an hour into the ride, the driver pulled off to the side of the road, screaming for the migrants to hide in the bushes. The coyote walked up ahead to investigate what he believed to be a major border patrol checkpoint in San Clemente, a strategic location often used by border patrol. Just fifty-four minutes north of San Diego, San Clemente was a notorious second line of the U.S. defense beyond its border with México. Without actually stopping vehicles, the San Clemente border allowed agents to conduct visual vehicle inspections from the checkpoint, as well as giving them the advantage to examine passenger's behaviors to gauge whether or not they might be crossing further into California without the proper documentation.

It was a false alarm, and my family resumed their cramped positions in the vehicle. Everyone was still emotionally and physically exhausted from the trip to San Diego and the lack of adequate food and water. Being wedged into a moving vehicle added more stress to their bodies. My family and the other migrants focused on their breathing, a task that proved to be difficult in their current positions on the car floor and trunk. Discomfort was a small price to pay in comparison to thousands of other migrants that had gone before and would go after my family. Thousands have lost their lives having suffocated in the trunks or backseats of crowded cars. Dead bodies have even been pulled from the back of crowded vans, without windows, that attempted to smuggle anywhere from forty to sixty people north at one time.

They arrived in Los Angeles during the early hours of the morning. My Tia Miriam and her husband were waiting for them on a street near her apartment building. Tia Miriam nervously handed the coyotes approximately $1,200 dollars, waiting for a reaction. She was still short with her final payment, despite the money she borrowed from neighbors and friends. The coyotes demanded the remainder of the funds, beginning to threaten my aunt and refusing to release my uncle still positioned inside the vehicle. Tio Robert was not allowed out of the vehicle until the full payment had been made to the coyotes. The coyotes had raised the final price without warning and would not allow for negotiation.

When promising over and over to pay as soon as she got the money didn't work, Tia Miriam pleaded with the lead coyote, asking him what else she might be able to provide for the release of her brother. In desperation, my aunt offered some of her most valuable items in exchange for my Tio Robert at the brink of suffocation in the shallow trunk of the long car. She retrieved a sewing machine and a majority of all her most prized jewelry for their release. In the blink of an eye, the coyotes left with items my aunt had saved for months and even years to purchase, and, just like that, it was all over. My family had made it to Los Angeles, California, where a new life awaited.

Welcome to Los Angeles

There is a miracle in every new beginning. — Hermann Hesse

My mother was mesmerized by the bright lights and tall buildings of Los Angeles. Life, in the beginning, was a big adjustment from her former existence in a small town in San Miguel. Things moved quickly in California, and my mother understood why the United States had a reputation for creating such wealth so quickly.

In Los Angeles, my mother's first job would be as a nanny taking care of kids in Pacoima, California, one of the oldest neighborhoods in the San Fernando Valley. The neighborhood was predominantly Mexican, so my mother was able to navigate with Spanish. The job only paid around thirty dollars a week, a sum hardly enough to get by.

She would only work with that family for a few months before she moved to another nanny job in Thousand Oaks, just north of L.A. in Ventura County, where the pay was almost three times what she was making in Pacoima. This was no surprise, as Thousand Oaks ranks as one of the richest cities in the United States.

As the nanny, my mother had a room in the house where she stayed five out of the seven days of the week. Aside from hating the long bus rides from Pico Union to her job in the next county, my mother missed being with family. She had never spent so much time apart from her siblings, and this ultimately prompted her to return to the small apartment near downtown Los Angeles.

My mother soon got a job in the fashion industry, where she worked in a warehouse that manufactured clothing for a number of popular brands. She would hold this job for almost three years before getting pregnant with me, her first child.

Like so many other migrants from Central America, my uncles found work in construction. These jobs varied depending on the amount of work every day. My uncles would compete with at least a dozen other men every morning, also determined to out-hustle their peers in exchange for getting paid. A paycheck was never guaranteed, and the men in the family often bounced around all over the city to wherever the work was available. They were all constantly looking over their shoulders as well, living with the fear that immigration services could show up at any time to arrest them for working undocumented. This was a risk my family had to take in order to pay rent and send money back to El Salvador.

Grandma Rosa Emília

I can do all things through Christ, who strengthens me. — Philippians 4:13

Rosa Emília Vasques was a loving mother who bore sixteen children, eight of which survived into adulthood. She was a hard worker from childhood, a wonderful cook, and an engaged member of the community. Rosa Emília loved to gamble, survived a civil war, and eventually migrated to the United States, where she would live in two different states. She was an explorer and, in her older years, would walk around Los Angeles daily. She was a living example of a strong Salvadoran woman. She had experienced much suffering but had no quit in her bones. She was relentless and wouldn't give up when she wanted something. Abuela Rosa Emília was one of the most driven and determined women in my entire family. She was our matriarch.

In El Salvador, it was common for men and women to rise before the sun, ready for the day's grind. Abuela Rosa Emília was a daughter of her culture and could trace her inauguration to hard work back to age five, where she helped her mother with work around the house and watching after her younger cousins and siblings. At age seven, she began leaving home to labor as a street vendor on the streets of El Salvador. By the time she was twelve years old, my grandmother was managing a food booth in the local *mercado* — market — of San Miguel, hand-making tortillas, and cooking rice, beans, and meat to serve full plates to local workers and families strolling through the city center at leisure.

Much of Rosa Emília's childhood was spent next to a *piedra para moler* — a stone carving for corn dough. She often joked with all of us, as she recounted stories later, that cooking tools were her everyday dolls and best friends growing up.

Rosa Emília spent her teenage years working side-by-side with her father, Concepción. Known around town as Don Concepción, her father was a tyrant at home. He was strict, seemingly without mercy, with every single one of his family

50

members, no matter their relation to him. Don Concepción's word was the law in his house, and disobedience would result in serious consequences for the offender. On occasions when family members, old and young, failed to greet him, he would lash out violently. Once he was in the comfort of his home, he would line up every single person in the backyard to whip them with a belt. It served everyone as a lesson that greeting him was an obligation they had to approach with humility.

Don Concepción's reputation and command for respect extended beyond the boundaries of his home. Don Concepción was a businessman with a sphere of influence over a few of the most fruitful parts of the local economy. He often walked around the streets of San Miguel and his family was obligated to stop what they were doing to greet him. Extending their hands, with their heads bowed down, both men and women would address him as *Bendito Papa Conce* — blessed father Conce — waiting for his nod of approval to dismiss them back to their duties. Failing to greet Papa Conce would mean punishment for every person once they got back home. He would sometimes require the family members that did not greet him properly to line up in the front yard to receive public belt thrashings. However, despite their strenuous relationship, Rosa Emília always had an unspoken bond with her father.

Papa Conce was something of a chief in San Miguel and everyone around him had to respect him. Disrespect or disapproval from Don Concepción also meant being dishonored and potentially being thrown into a life of extreme poverty. Many of the men and women in his immediate family depended on Don Concepción's businesses for work in order to provide for their own families. Disrespecting him could mean that you were no longer employed in the blink of an eye.

As my grandmother grew older, she thought more about her future. She dreamed of getting married and starting a new life dictated by her own choices, far away from her father's draconian household. In San Miguel, marriage was almost the only way a woman could leave her family's home.

Like all things in his universe, Don Concepción wanted to be in control, and that meant choosing the man each one of his daughters would marry. Marriage for Don Concepción was a business transaction. Therefore, all of the men on his list were older and wealthy. He wanted their maturity and money to provide his daughters and their children with financial stability. My grandmother entertained the men her father presented to keep his temper at bay. However, she never loved any of the men and promised herself that she would never actually marry them. Rosa Emília was persistent in her focus on choosing her own future. After many failed attempts to find my grandmother a wealthy suitor, my great-grandfather Don Concepción reluctantly allowed Rosa Emília to marry a man of her own choosing.

At the age of nineteen, Rosa Emília wed Luis Moreno, a talented musician and a good-looking man about ten years her senior. Luis, athletically thin, with dark curly hair, had a smile that melted most women right away. Rosa Emília, contrary to her initial resistance, felt like she had finally met the man that could rescue her from her father's severe rule over her life. Luis Moreno had charm and wit. He was adventurous and made up for his shortcomings with language that could make any woman feel like the only one in the room. His charm hooked my grandmother, and she fought hard with Don Concepción for his approval.

Luis Moreno was the opposite of what Don Concepción wanted for his daughter. He was a struggling artist with little money and influence in the music community. He eventually conceded, and their marriage allowed my grandmother to leave her childhood home. Don Concepción's authorization of their union, however, was not absolute, and Rosa Emília left with dishonor. As a clear demonstration of his power, Don Concepción would pay for Rosa Emília's wedding, but it would be the last thing he would do for her before her departure. He would then disown my grandmother, and without his protection and support, she would live a life of extreme poverty and hardship.

How It All Started

Luis Moreno and Rosa Emília met at a wedding of mutual friends. Rosa Emília had been convinced to go to the wedding by her friend and was barely engaged in conversation with other guests when she noticed a man looking at her from the other side of the room. She turned her back toward him, uninterested in speaking to any more people than she had to at the event she was forced to attend.

At some point during the afternoon, Luis boldly approached my grandmother and expressed his interest in her. Already a mother of two, Rosa Emília promptly told Luis that she was no longer a child and that she had no interest in silly games. She had never been married before but had been in a relationship with a man named Antonio for almost four years. It was during that time that she bore a son, Antonio, known as *Toño*, and a daughter, Miriam. After finding Antonio in bed with another woman, Rosa Emília called it quits and never looked back. Now, as a single mother of two, she had no time for nonsense. Rosa Emília wanted to find a suitable husband and father to her children so that she could leave Don Concepción's home. She was beautiful but pragmatic. Rosa Emília had responsibilities and a vision for her life. Luis acknowledged her candid response with his intent to marry her and start a family together.

In the beginning, things were great. Luis was loyal and built Rosa Emília three houses with aluminum and other cheap material, as was common in El Salvador. This honeymoon period was short-lived, however, and soon his charming wit that made him so attractive turned to violence and indifference toward Rosa Emília. Their marriage would last twenty-five years, a period of great instability and inconsistent emotion for my grandmother Rosa Emília. Over the years, the beatings would grow more frequent and more violent. In one of his most cruel acts of brutality, Luis Moreno tied my grandmother to a tree in front of the house and beat her until she was unconscious. He intended to not only hurt her physically that day but also to humiliate her in front of her neighbors.

The time Luis spent outside their home increased as his unfaithful nature lent him to up to two or three other women at a time. Rosa Emília would walk to the local mercado and, more and more frequently, see Luis walking in the opposite direction with another woman on his arm. She would eventually confirm that Luis Moreno had fathered almost ten other children outside of their marriage.

After more than two decades of marriage, my grandmother left Luis, taking eight of their children along with her. Luis Junior was the only child that stayed behind to be raised by his paternal grandmother. Throughout the 1970s, Luis Moreno continued his life as a musician and moved around El Salvador for work. Rosa Emília didn't see him for years after she left, and she focused on providing for her family as a food vendor. Eventually, Luis Moreno reappeared. He asked for favors and free food from the business my grandmother had grown to support the children he had abandoned.

Against her rationality and better judgment, Rosa Emília took Luis Moreno back in and cared for him. At this point, the civil war had started, and my mother, aunt, and uncle had already departed for California. Feeling the need to keep her community together in some way, my grandmother found a way to put aside the pain Luis had caused her. However, his presence wouldn't last, and they again parted ways. Rosa Emília would eventually make the decision to follow her family to Los Angeles a few years later.

On her migration journey to Los Angeles with my Tio Oscar, now an experienced coyote, Rosa Emília would cross paths with Luis Moreno once again in Chiapas, México, just a few weeks after she had left El Salvador. Luis was also making his way to the United States. This would be his second time going north. His first trip to Los Angeles was funded by Rosa Emília's daughters — my mother and Tia Miriam. He had only stayed a few weeks in California before heading back to El Salvador to ask for financial support from my grandmother. Luis Moreno opposed hard work in every way, and finding himself in a foreign land with few acquaintances, he gave up quickly and returned to San Miguel.

In Chiapas, Luis was leading his own group of six people to the U.S. With little money and experience, he was broke by the time he got to México, once again needing his family's support. The group had now almost doubled, with Tia Miriam taking on an unexpected financial burden. By the time they arrived in Oaxaca, there was no money left for anyone, which forced the group to settle there for three months while Miriam found enough money to send for their continued travels. In Oaxaca, a local Christian pastor would provide all fourteen travelers with a small space they would call home for months. Abuela Rosa Emília became the unofficial cook of the group during that time, ensuring everyone had something to eat, including her ex-husband. Luis Moreno remained quiet most of those months. However, he continued to accept every hot meal he was served.

From Oaxaca, the group would make their way to Ciudad de México — México City — by passenger trains. The Mexican capital was the place my mother, Sandra, had spent a couple of months in the home of the García family years before. Tio Oscar always enjoyed reconnecting with Ciudad de México, a city that welcomed him during his first attempt north. This time, they would only pass through the bustling center in order to catch a bus headed to Guadalajara. After so much time lost in the southern part of México, Oscar hoped it would be a passing of good fortune.

Once in México City, Oscar would not experience his normal welcome and ease of travel through the city. The group was stopped by the police under suspicion that they weren't locals. The Mexican authorities, uninterested in making any arrests, extorted my uncle for money and watches he had purchased in Guatemala in exchange for the group's freedom. The México City experience of essentially being robbed by the police was a bittersweet moment for Tio Oscar. He had once felt such a strong connection with the city that he would now rush to leave.

The bus ride to Guadalajara would be the most difficult part of the journey for my family. The ten adults and four teenagers of the group would hop on *La Bestia* — the beast — the cheapest and fastest transportation option for the group, to get to the

North American border. La Bestia was a freight train meant to carry cargo through México, not humans, but with little money and resources for a group that size, Oscar and Robert were left with few options. They would sneak aboard the freight train and ride the infamous *el tren de la muerte* — train of death — as it was popularly called, through Central México.

The women of the group, including Abuela Rosa Emília, were hidden inside of empty barrels being transported. While their limbs would go numb from being confined in such a tight space for a long period of time, Tio Oscar and Tio Robert needed to protect the women from bandits who were known for hopping on board the freight train and raping women migrants. To further protect the group, the men would arm themselves with sticks and rocks they picked up along the way, forming a barrier around the women and hiding them from any and all criminals. As La Bestia moved through the darkness during the evenings, the men had very few opportunities to sleep, staying awake to keep watch of anyone coming from the front or back of the train that could attempt to harm them.

Over the next five days, the group would complete the train ride in silence. They had to remain quiet to avoid being caught and avoid any passing criminals that were looking to rob or rape vulnerable travelers. Tio Oscar only spoke to tell the group to get ready when it was time to get off. La Bestia had multiple stops along the way to deliver cargo and refuel. At each stop, the group would have an hour, just barely enough time to get some food and back on the train safely. At a few stops along the way, the group had to run and hide from local police, which prevented them from getting anything to eat. After those stops, the group would sometimes go full days without a meal.

Arriving in Mexicali, the group would finally finish their travels on La Bestia, *el tren de la muerte,* and would eventually board a bus to Tijuana. Once there, only fifteen miles from the U.S. border, the group would have to wait another two months for additional money from Tia Miriam before finally crossing over into Los Angeles and beginning their new life in the U.S.

In 1990, Abuela Rosa Emília was living in Los Angeles, California. I was five years old at the time and spent a lot of time at her apartment with my two sisters to escape the physical abuse of my mother by my stepfather. So much time in my grandmother's home allowed me to develop a strong bond with Abuela Rosa Emília. As a child, I rarely ever left her side, thus never missed a story about her life back in El Salvador. I learned about her life cooking for others to make a living, her gambling stories, and her many intricately detailed tales about escaping danger and sometimes death in search of a better life for her family.

My grandmother on her way to church. She attended service several times a week to give thanks and to pray for our family.

When I was around six years old, my grandmother received the terrible news that her father, Don Concepción, was dying of cirrhosis and that he had requested to see Abuela Rosa Emília one last time before he died. It had been almost ten years since they had last spoken in person, and Rosa Emília, like Don Concepción, wanted to clear the air before he died.

Without consulting any of her eight children, my grandmother bought a one-way plane ticket back to El Salvador to sit by her father's bedside. My grandmother was to fly back to her homeland to reunite with her family and care for her father one last time. After years of feuding over disagreements, Concepción needed to ask for forgiveness before dying.

Our entire family accompanied my grandmother to the airport. Aunts, uncles, cousins, and my mother all took turns hugging Abuela Rosa Emília, not knowing if we would ever see her again. The legal status of almost all of my family members, including my grandmother, prevented them from leaving and re-entering the U.S. If she decided to return to Los Angeles, it would mean one more life-threatening voyage back over the border. This would be something for her to accomplish at almost fifty years old, after putting her father to rest.

Upon arrival in San Miguel, Abuela Rosa Emília learned that her father, Don Concepción's health had rapidly declined even further. The same man who once pointed a gun at a corn mill owner to save the last two fingers left on my mother's mangled hand was now a frail, old man lying in bed for his final days. Don Concepción could barely keep a steady rhythm of breath as he waited to see his favorite daughter one last time. Throughout their turbulent relationship, they still maintained that special connection. Even during times when they were not speaking, they always seemed to know what the other was doing from afar. Their tumultuous history of his strict ways and disapproval of her choices no longer mattered to my Abuela Rosa Emília. She just wanted to be with her father.

After a few months in San Miguel, Abuela Rosa Emília laid her father to rest. They had endured over ten years without communication, but she had peace with their reconciliation at the end of his life. She was able to say goodbye to Don Concepción, the strict man of her earliest years, who taught her hard work and had inadvertently pushed her in search of her own life and dreams.

Don Concepción's death brought closure to my grandmother. She stayed in El Salvador for another year to support the family and attend to the final affairs of her father's business, but Rosa Emília knew that her life was no longer in El Salvador, and it was soon time to head back to the United States.

Against All Odds

Thirteen months after her father's death, Rosa Emília was ready to return to her children and grandchildren in Los Angeles. Tio Robert had left the Salvadoran military, secured legal American documentation, and was now an experienced coyote, helping other family members and neighbors get into the U.S. in search of a better life. He would soon be making a trip to El Salvador to lead a new group of family members to the U.S., including my Abuela Rosa Emília.

When my grandmother first expressed her wish to head back north, Tio Robert was very reluctant to give a response. He could never say no to Rosa Emília as our family's matriarch, but he also understood the danger ahead of them. He stalled as long as he could to avoid giving her an answer. My grandmother's health was declining, and she was at an older age. Running away from border police in the middle of the night was not a fate Tio Robert and the family even wanted to consider in thinking about Rosa Emília's journey north.

To make matters worse, Tio Robert had noticed my grandmother had become overweight after a year of indulging in the best food El Salvador had to offer. After so long of being in the United States, my grandmother never declined an offer to eat and celebrate with her friends in her native land. However, Tio Robert eventually agreed after my grandmother, an extremely stubborn woman, would not take no for an answer. Staying in San Miguel wasn't an option for her, and she was determined to make it back to L.A. one way or another.

To prepare herself physically for the journey, Rosa Emília would make athlete-like changes in her life by her own account. She trained like an athlete by walking and running long distances around all of San Miguel to build endurance. She would often remind our family of her strength during this time, proudly recounting her disciplined workouts in her determination to get back to us in Los Angeles. At over fifty years old, Rosa Emília would return home, drenched in sweat from a run around her city, as she put her body through the rigorous workouts that would bring her closer to accomplishing her goal.

As a sports fan, I think back to my grandmother's running, and I am reminded of track and field runner Heather Dornidon. Heather was a collegiate champion who rose to fame after one 800-meter race. In the middle of the race, Heather tripped and fell to the ground dramatically, giving all the other runners the notion that the race was over. Instead, Heather got back up, determined to recover the enormous amount of time she had lost with her fall. Dornidon took off like a rocket and began closing the gap one foot at a time. The announcers were in shock as she moved past each runner and won the race.

Rosa Emília wasn't running an 800-meter race. This was a 3,000-mile event where even the smallest trip or mistake could cost you your freedom or even your life.

My understanding of situations typically goes to sports; hence the Heather Dornidon comparison, and my grandmother helped instill that in me. She would constantly remind us that life was a long race, not a 100-yard sprint.

Both lessons share the same sentiment — the desire to achieve something amazing. Greatness is bred from an unparalleled level of desire. When you want something bad enough, you're willing to go through things you never imagined you could endure. Much like Dornidon wanted to win that race, despite her pain and exhaustion, my grandmother wanted to get back to Los Angeles regardless of the price. My Abuela Rosa Emília was willing to be uncomfortable in her training and, eventually, to put her life on the line to get back to what was most important to her.

The trip to the U.S. wasn't going to be cheap, and my grandmother had spent all of her savings to get back to San Miguel and to support her father and family leading up to and after Don Concepción's death. Times were difficult financially for the rest of the family in Los Angeles as well, which made it unclear whether or not her children could help Rosa Emília get back to the States. As a converted Christian, Rosa Emília's faith kept her dream strong, and she continued to pray, believing that something would allow her trip to become a reality. Rosa Emília's recipe of faith and determination was enough to convince her that the dominos would fall in her favor sooner rather than later.

Days before Tio Robert's group would be departing north, local family members in San Miguel invited Abuela Rosa Emília over to wish her luck on the journey and to say goodbye. One by one, different family members would pull Rosa Emília to the side and hand her a fist full of rolled-up bills, jewelry, and other valuables they had been saving to support her along the way. By the end of the evening, my grandmother had received one thousand dollars in cash for her trip, in addition to a number of gold rings and watches. While Rosa Emília still did not have enough money for the journey across El Salvador, Guatemala, and México, she took her good fortune as a sign from God that she was on the right track. Abuela Rosa Emília gave Tio Robert half of the money she had been gifted and kept the other half to buy her own food along the way. She remembered how long the periods of hunger could last from their last trip riding La Bestia, and she hoped to be better prepared and to keep her strength up this time around.

After only one day into their trip, Rosa Emília began questioning if her body could handle the entire journey. Her physical training had allowed her to lose the weight that would have weighed her down, but the long days without sleep or stability were mentally taxing in ways that were more difficult than anything she could have prepared for. Following the route Tio Oscar had taken a decade earlier, Robert led the new group through small towns, depending heavily on local help to keep the group safe and healthy.

After short stops throughout Guatemala and Chiapas, the group was advancing north faster than expected. They would make their first official resting stop to stay with the same Christian family in Oaxaca who had taken them in years earlier. The group would stay in Oaxaca for over a week. Although it was much less time than Rosa Emília's first visit, there was something different about her time in Oaxaca on this trip. Rosa Emília was taken by the peacefulness and humbleness of the people in the city. Instantly, she developed relationships and was even asked to stay by her newly found community. When it was finally time for the group to leave, locals gathered to say farewell to Rosa Emília as if they were lifetime friends. She was sent off with baskets filled with food to last her for the next couple of days. This was another sign from God along her journey, demonstrated through the kindness of the Oaxacan people — a sign of goodwill experienced by many immigrants traveling from Central America.

Leaving Oaxaca, the group would continue north the fastest way possible, riding La Bestia, the same freight train known for killing hundreds of immigrants along the way and the same train that had invoked a gripping fear in my grandmother years earlier. This second time around, however, Rosa Emília wasn't afraid of La Bestia. Like an established enemy, Rosa Emília felt a sense of peaceful fear climbing back onto the train. She was reminded of all she had lived through: her country's civil war, a violent and painful marriage, a trip like this once before, and, most recently, the passing of her father. Rosa Emília scaled the frail, swaying ladder of the train with her eyes fixed as far out as her vision would let her. She knew she could do this again.

The ride on La Bestia was less intimidating hiding in the barrel as an older woman this time around. The threat of bandits on the train was still there but seemed to pose less risk for Rosa Emília than the stops along the way in unknown towns with unexpected challenges waiting for them. Thoughts of not running fast enough back to the train and being left behind in the middle of nowhere plagued my grandmother. Despite her fear, my grandmother had made a commitment to never complain along this trip. It didn't matter if she was hungry or thirsty; she moved along with the group and only stopped when everyone else did. That faith that had afforded her this far in her journey back to her family kept her focused on making it into Tijuana and then across the border.

Upon arriving in Tijuana, a coyote hired by Tio Robert was already waiting for Rosa Emília and three others to cross to San Diego. My grandmother's training in San Miguel would now be put to the test for their miles-long walk over the border. They waited for hours in the bushes for nightfall to come and the coyote to deem their path clear.

Rosa Emília prayed for the group's safety in traveling across the border the entire time. She called on the faith that had brought her to this moment once again to bring them into the final and most difficult leg of the trip. When she finally made it into California, Rosa Emília looked up in the sky and thanked the heavens for letting her do the unthinkable twice. Whenever asked about this trip, my grandmother would lead the story by thanking God.

A vision of a life in the north willed into existence by faith, prayer and determination brought my family together in Los Angeles. Our story is similar to that of thousands of immigrants that have worked their way into the U.S. for a better life. Much like my Abuela Rosa Emília, these families saw their future before they lived it. Life wasn't always good to my grandmother, but her vision and grit led her to a life she had created in her mind long before. It was a dream that had been placed in her heart amidst a brutal civil war and a cheating husband. With consistent gratitude, my grandmother would send money back to San Miguel from California for more than thirty years until her dying days.

Listening to my grandmother's migration story to the United States would later become the blueprint for how I approached things I wanted in life. I would visualize the outcome before it became a reality. In order to understand where I was headed in life, I had to comprehend my family's history and the reasons behind their decision to come to the U.S. At the very least, I needed to get to know the two women who raised me.

In 2012, Abuela Rosa Emília was living in Houston, Texas, with my Tia Miriam. After traveling part of her life between Houston and Los Angeles, my grandmother decided she wanted to stay in L.A. permanently to be close to a majority of the family. Three months after her move, Abuela Rosa Emília was informed that she had cirrhosis, the same illness that took her father's life. After a doctor's visit my grandmother was already reluctant to attend, doctors informed her that her illness was terminal and that she had, at most, six months to live.

At this time, I was living on the East Coast, working on making my own dreams a reality. Upon hearing the news, I immediately boarded a plane to sit at my grandmother's side. For the almost six-hour plane ride, I was overcome with sadness and the reality that this could be the last time I would ever see my grandmother. I formulated a million questions to ask her and wondered how I would get through them all if her time with us was limited. Arriving at my aunt's house and seeing the feeble condition my grandmother was in prompted me to make time with her my priority for as long as she was alive.

Over the next few weeks, I sat by my grandmother's bedside and learned more about her life and the history of our family. As the matriarch of our family, she was a human library with an infinite number of stories. Listening to the grit and determination in each of her tales, I couldn't help but wonder if I possessed the same persistence to achieve my goals and dreams.

In 2014, Abuela Rosa Emília passed away. While I was grateful for the time I was able to spend with her in her dying days, I was devastated. I had learned so much from her, but it seemed like her passing came too soon. Our family often even had a running joke, before she got sick, that she was so strong that she would probably live to 100 years old. It was in that moment of thinking about our family joke that I was reminded of a lesson she had taught me. In difficult moments and situations, both my grandmother and mother always saw the good that could come out of bad times. Being women of strong faith, they would constantly repeat that God allowed things to happen for a reason.

Remembering that lesson while remembering her brought me instant comfort. I knew that through the life lessons she gave me,

I would never be without her. Her stories, memories, and lessons would live inside of me. There would be something big that came out of this tragedy.

My City

To live and die in L.A., it's the place to be. You've got to be there to know it, when everybody wanna see. — Tupac

Los Angeles is more than the city where I was born and raised. The city taught me what real strength was by showing me how to survive. South Central showed me the life I did not want which somehow gave me the chance to dream beyond my block.

At five years old, I held a real gun for the first time. Unable to fully comprehend what I had in my hands, I thought it was cool. I thought I was powerful. The gun was my stepfather's 9-millimeter. I wanted to be just like him and all of his friends that walked around strapped in the streets.

While we sometimes got the strict Christian version of him, most of the time, my stepfather would return home drunk after days and sometimes weeks of being gone. When he was around, he would be hanging out with the homies in our neighborhood in front of the house or along the back alleyway.

Our home was filled with violence when my stepfather was around, but danger was also waiting for me outside of our four walls. The streets of South Central ran rampant with gangs, drugs, and violence. On more than one occasion, God's mercy protected me from harm's way, and I found myself lucky to be alive.

South Central, Los Angeles was never an easy place to navigate, but I've maintained that if I could survive those streets, I could overcome anything in life.

Just like my family, L.A. is home to some of the hardest working people in the country. The city is filled with immigrants from México and many Central American countries. Unless you were born into wealth, you learned to hustle from a very young age. Our version of Los Angeles wasn't Hollywood and glamor. Instead, this was the city where anyone who wanted something bad enough had to work hard to make it happen.

El Barrio — the neighborhood or hood — was run by street vendors working daily to make ends meet. Every morning you heard the food vendors yelling *"tamales"* to sell to workers in the area, while *los paleteros* — ice cream salesmen — rang the bells of their little carts and walked down the streets of each neighborhood shouting *paletas! raspados!* — ice cream — every afternoon. All the local neighborhood kids would run behind them waving their dollar bills, ready to ask for their favorite flavor.

Growing up, I spent much of my time where Slauson Avenue met Crenshaw Boulevard and the Pico Union area near downtown L.A. Pico Union was a part of Los Angeles where hundreds of Salvadorans and other Central Americans arrived during the 1980s to escape civil unrest. It was one of the few affordable areas near downtown.

With a population of over 40,000 residents, it wasn't rare for my aunts and uncles to run into people they knew back in El Salvador. Pico Union defined my years as an elementary school student, and its neighborhood culture molded my emotional and intellectual development. The community created a humility in me that I saw from so many working so hard to feed their families. It also kept my Salvadoran roots alive within me.

It was also in Pico Union, however, where I first saw drugs being sold. Eventually, I would learn that my stepfather sold drugs, waiting for his customers only a few houses down from our front door. This is why he carried a gun and was always spending time outside.

When I got a little older, I was asked to run drugs from our building to a random stranger's car. The first time I carried a package outside for him, the drugs were inside a spare diaper from my little sister. My stepfather never seemed to respect the boundaries of keeping the family safe, which I quickly learned as I got older.

Pico Union was also the heart of gang wars. Street battles and drive-by shootings would take many young men away from family and friends, including friends and family members of mine.

Living in South Central, my mother made it a priority to make sure I developed a thick skin to survive the violent and chaotic neighborhoods where we often lived. Just being perceived as weak made you a target for gang members or bullies looking to rob and attack someone for street credit or "cred." Her lessons would help keep us alive if we ever found ourselves in dangerous situations, and they were ones she pulled from the violence of her childhood in El Salvador.

With my stepfather's inconsistency, my mother took on the tasks usually secured by the man of the house. This included tips to keep us safe and stand up for ourselves. Despite having three uncles and the husbands of my mother's sisters around, the men in our family never seemed to be around enough during hard times. This forced me to grow up faster than most kids.

My mother worked and stayed long hours away from home to provide for me, my brother, and my five sisters. From around the age of six, I helped take care of my younger siblings while my mother was gone.

Unusual and undocumented in the United States, this form of childcare was necessary in order for my mother to save money and continue to put food on the table. Caring for my younger siblings strengthened my bonds with my sisters Ingrid, Karla, Jennifer, Joana, Elkhen, and my brother Abraham. I got to know them in a different light and care for each one of them like a father care for a child. I watched over them, played with them, and cooked our meals when my mom was out working.

Los Angeles is a beautiful city, but there are parts of the city where one wrong turn can land you into a gang or drug lord territory running for your life. Ending up on an unknown street could get you "hit up," where you will be approached and asked about your gang affiliation. These minor and casual hit-ups ended with a stabbing or shooting on multiple occasions. Hit-ups happened all the time on my block. I witnessed countless strangers, just passing through the neighborhood, get robbed or beaten.

Drive-by shootings were also common on my block. As kids, we learned how to hit the ground and cover your head to avoid gunshots. These were things we learned as soon as we could walk. In the early '90s, we lived in an apartment with a window facing the street, which made us vulnerable to gangs driving by to spray anyone in rival territory with bullets.

At least twice a month, the sound of gunshots would blast through our home. The Mara Salvatrucha, also known as MS-13, and the 18th street gangs ruled the Pico Union community and were often at war with each other. Over the years, people we knew in the neighborhood weren't lucky enough to survive the violence. We had several neighbors whose sons and daughters were gunned down as innocent bystanders. This was a normal part of our reality.

In 1991, headlines at the Los Angeles Times would report record numbers of more than 700 gang-affiliated deaths. During the 1990s, homicides were nearing 2,000 per year. Almost half of those murders were attributed to gang violence. People became desensitized to those losses. When someone was murdered, we placed a candle at the location to honor their life and then kept moving. These small tributes to honor and pray for those we loved and lost could be found all around Pico Union.

Only ten years after fleeing a vicious war in El Salvador and arriving in L.A., my family had entered another battleground. A gang war in the streets of L.A. and tension between law enforcement and communities of color was at its boiling point for a second time in fifty years.

The Riots

The Los Angeles Riots of 1992 left a scar on the psyche of thousands of Angelinos. It is a historical event that has stayed with me my entire life. It was the deadliest year of Los Angeles' growing homicide rate at the beginning of the 1990s. Over 2,500 murders happened in one year due to gang violence and a surge of weapons on the street.

Tensions between the Los Angeles Police Department and communities of color in the city were as high as ever. Especially after a Black man named Rodney King was brutally beaten by four officers a year prior. Just two weeks later, 15-year-old Latasha Harlins would be shot in the back of the head by a Korean small market owner who had assumed Harlins was stealing. This was a demonstration of the tension that existed even among communities of color, as Korean families set up businesses in Black neighborhoods yet allowed their fear of that very community to be fueled by racist stereotypes. The Black community could trace this type of systemic harassment in the city well beyond the footage of 1991. The Watts Riots of 1965 left over thirty people dead, along with millions of dollars' worth of property damages.

In 1992, I had just turned seven years old and I had very little understanding of what was taking place in Los Angeles. Like many families with a television, I remember seeing the clips of Rodney King's beating played on a loop. After fifty-six blows by the batons of the officers, King would suffer eleven fractures in addition to countless other injuries to his face and body. It was one of the first times many of us would see the police brutality our neighborhood endured on a daily basis broadcast over national television. On April 29th, 1992, the King verdict would trigger a city-wide protest after the four white officers involved were acquitted of any crime. After seven days of deliberations by an almost all-white jury, disappointment at the injustice of the decision erupted in Los Angeles. You could hear the shouting in anger and disagreement inside of my building. Our predominantly Latino neighborhood had also suffered years of unjust policing, and the pain of the decision passed through all of us.

L.A. Mayor Tom Bradley held a press conference after the trial's conclusion and confirmed for the nation what we already knew.

"Today, the jury told the world that what we all saw with our own eyes was not a crime. My friends, I am here to tell the jury... what we saw was a crime. No, we will not tolerate the savage beating of our citizens by a few renegade cops." - Tom Bradley, Mayor of Los Angeles 1973-1993

Hours after the mayor's press conference, news reports of protests in front of the courthouse around South Central, Los Angeles, and Koreatown replaced the Rodney King beating on TV. Normandie and Florence Avenues, south of downtown L.A. and only twenty minutes away from our apartment, had become the most dangerous intersection for any driver who wasn't Black, as a white truck driver was pulled from his car and beaten close to death by a crowd of angry Angelinos. Chaos followed with fires, store windows being busted in, and looting. It was all caught on video by local TV news stations and civilians with recording cameras that captured moments TV crews missed.

The turmoil spread throughout the city. I feared that our building would be burned in the community's own frustration. It wasn't long before the skies over Los Angeles grew dark as the smoke from the fires covered parts of the city. My family referred to this period often as *la quemazon* — the fires. Aside from the protests and fires, my most vivid memory was watching people loot businesses. People were running out of stores with anything they could carry. It seemed to me that some Angelinos were standing up against police brutality, injustice, and racial discrimination, while others simply saw an opportunity to steal.

For everyone in my neighborhood, Rodney King's video was a reminder about our place in Los Angeles. Living in Pico Union meant that we experienced violence at both the hands of the authorities and the gangs. The events of 1992 reminded us that our community was so often neglected, both with resources and

71

justice from the law. Our people weren't treated the same as other parts of the city and we saw ourselves in Mr. King. Soon after the riots began, the men of my extended family decided to join other Latinos, Asian Americans, whites, and African Americans who protested.

Coming from a war-torn country, they understood what it was like to be harassed by men in uniforms. They weren't alone; many young adults from the neighborhood tagged along. The Latino community would be heavily represented in the L.A. Riots, making up 51% of the 10,000 arrests during the period of protest during the '90s.

Hundreds of people walked the streets of Los Angeles frustrated with the system that was meant to protect them yet only oppressed them further. Extensive conversations and arguments broke out amongst my neighbors, most infuriated by watching the King video. Everyone seemed to agree that the LAPD was not on our side. This rage translated into more than 1,000 buildings around Los Angeles being destroyed or damaged.

I watched people in my neighborhood burglarize big and small businesses, and it made me question the integrity of our people. Korean-Latino businesses all over south L.A. weren't exempt from the looting. The absence of police in some areas of the city caused some Korean store owners to take extreme safety measures, which only fueled the riots. Store owners carried guns and stealing from the wrong store could get you shot. It was a terrifying time. My mother, siblings, and I watched neighbors return home with boxes of stolen merchandise daily. These were wild days and people operated without fear of consequences.

My uncles were among those stealing from local spots. They looted electronic stores in hopes of reselling things in the streets. It was an easy way to make some money. When things finally began to settle down, my stepfather took me on a scavenger hunt around the neighborhood without my mother's consent. Several businesses had been broken into the night prior, and people were up early the next morning looking for something to steal, including my stepfather.

We weren't the only people with that same idea so early in the morning. We were met at the storefront by a decent-sized crowd of others looking for anything useful to take. Just being around other people made me nervous. I had seen the crowds on TV, and I was unsure of what could happen. My stepfather led me through the building remains, telling me to stay close. To his disappointment, there wasn't much left to take by the time we arrived. Even the doors and portions of the roof were missing at that point. One of the walls had even collapsed. The building was falling apart, and you could see smoke coming out from the fire that had been extinguished hours before. All we found that day were some dusty bags of soap that might've been worth a few dollars.

Unwilling to accept that the trip was a bad idea from the beginning, my stepfather handed me the bags of soap to carry, and we ventured further up the street to see what else we could find. Our local video store was less than a block up, and we saw people leaving with arms full of movies. My stepfather told me to wait outside and was in and out of the video rental store with a box of VHS tapes. He had stolen the entire Bruce Lee collection, knowing exactly where they were located.

We were normal customers at the rental store and always said hello to the staff. I was terrified to say anything to my stepfather, but I felt terrible for the owner. I imagined he had worked very hard for his business, and I enjoyed seeing him when our family went to rent movies.

When we got back home, my mother lost it and began screaming at my stepfather, angry that he had put me in harm's way. She made it clear that he was free to do what he pleased with his own life but not with mine. He had put us both at risk for some dusty soap and karate movies.

I didn't really understand what I was living through in Los Angeles until I was much older. The riots were fundamental in strengthening my character during a difficult period in L.A. history. Like many other kids my age who lived in the

73

neighborhood, this historical event was a crossroads on how we would choose to behave during difficult times. I had family members, including my beloved uncles, that stole significant amounts of electronics and other goods during the looting. They sold the stolen TVs, blenders, and radios on our block before the police caught them during post-riot looting raids.

My cousins and I, at only seven and eight years old, were debating on whether or not to steal from our local liquor store because we saw others doing it. Some of my cousins chose to steal, and I couldn't understand why. Perhaps because they saw our uncles doing it. I cannot say. As young men growing up, we were conflicted about our own behavior. Would we listen to our mothers and avoid trouble and stealing? Or would we follow in the footsteps of our uncles and fathers, the men of our family whom we loved and greatly respected, and make decisions with heavy consequences? In the end, I knew my mother would be disappointed with me, and I always chose to stay back and observe quietly.

While decisions about my own behavior impacted my day-to-day development, I also began to understand the history of systemic and institutional racism in the United States. As I got older, I understood that people that looked like my Tio Oscar or Rodney King were treated differently — unjustly most of the time. I was proud that my community stood up in outrage against the unjust beating of a Black man and general police brutality, despite the tensions that sometimes existed between people of color. Regardless of those whose behavior was questionable, I was glad to see my community step up in the name of justice. From El Barrio to the riots, Los Angeles was shaping me, transforming me into the man I was destined to become.

Elementary

Have I not commanded you? Be strong and courageous. Do not be frightened, and do not be dismayed, for the Lord your God is with you wherever you go.
—Joshua 1:9

Faith played a prominent role throughout my life in helping me to overcome the most difficult moments. As a kid growing up in a Christian family, Joshua 1:9 was the first biblical verse I learned. My Abuela Rosa Emília and my mother would teach me to repeat Joshua 1:9 to eliminate any fear I might have, no matter the situation.

They taught me to speak with God and to understand His word as a command over my life. My connection with God created a voice and guide within me that allowed me to push forward in situations that seemed impossible to overcome.

I was teased sometimes as a child, and people would make comments about my family's status. My mother, not a novice at building a thick skin after losing three fingers in a work accident as a child, would use our faith to build my inner strength. She spoke of a greater purpose, God's greater purpose, for my life. My mother would tell me that she believed our family survived violence and traveled far just to bring me here to lay a new foundation for generations to come. I soaked these words in, surprisingly never fearful of the weight they held for me. My mother's prophecy over my life fueled me. Her words and my faith would shape my inner voice of motivation from childhood into adulthood.

I attended Magnolia Elementary on South Orchard Avenue, right across the street from my grandmother's apartment. I could always see home during recess and often spotted ambulances pulling up to the front of our house to transport my Tio Milton to a nearby hospital.

Tio Milton was sick with diabetes and had developed elephantiasis, which caused him to be in and out of the hospital. Milton was a smooth character and I looked up to him as a child. It was difficult to see him in pain and watched how he lay in bed, helpless. After school, I would sit by his bedside and listen to his stories about life before his illness. He would always tell me that no matter what happened, I could always make my dreams come true if I worked hard enough at something and continued to believe. Tio Milton lived with Abuela Rosa Emília to help care for and protect her. He wanted to make sure she was well taken care of before he started a family of his own, which never came to fruition for him. He instilled in me that I had to do something big and "be somebody" when I grew up in order to help my mother.

After a few years of battling with his illness, Tio Milton was hospitalized for several days. Eventually, he was put on life support, and, as his health worsened, my family was faced with a tough decision of whether or not to keep him alive on machines.

I heard the news coming back from the liquor store with my cousin Gilberto, and we felt the sadness filling the house as soon as we walked into Abuela Rosa Emília's apartment. When they decided to remove Tio Milton's life support, it was the first time I saw my entire family cry, grieving for such a tremendous and generous loss of life. My grandmother was crushed. Not only had she lost a son, but she had also very little saved to pay for Tio Milton's body to be flown back to El Salvador for a proper burial in his homeland.

My grandmother worked sporadically when it was necessary, but at her age, she mostly relied on her children to support her. Any additional income Abuela Rosa Emília earned was typically sent back to her family and friends in El Salvador (in 2019, almost 21% of El Salvador's GDP was made up of personal remittances). No one in my family had a large sum of money like that saved.

Our family did what so many other Central Americans did in our neighborhood when in need. We asked neighbors, friends, and even strangers for any financial help they might be able to provide, no matter how small the amount. Abuela Rosa Emília remained composed throughout the entire process of gathering small sums of money to add to our larger burial fund. She never lost sight of her desire to bury her son back in San Miguel. This was the second time Rosa Emília had lost a son. Her firstborn had been murdered back in El Salvador due to a domestic dispute with a married woman's family almost twenty years earlier. Despite her stoic posture during the fundraising process, I caught her crying a few times when she thought no one was looking. These small, secret moments were ones that only I got to witness. When family was around, she showed her strength and inspired hope in us all, but I was close enough to truly see her.

After a few weeks of knocking on doors and petitioning friends, the streets of Los Angeles had provided enough funds to buy two tickets, one for my Tio Robert and another for Milton's body, to El Salvador, where Milton would be buried. Abuela Rosa Emília would not return to her homeland again because of her legal status. After two dangerous trips and her older age, Rosa Emília would remain in the United States for the rest of her life.

It was in that final goodbye that I stood in front of Tio Milton's casket that I suddenly understood what was really happening. This was the first time I had ever lost someone close to me. Months went by and I couldn't stop thinking that Tio Milton was gone forever. Everywhere, space around the apartment reminded me of him, and it was hard not to constantly feel the void of his death. My family, always driven by faith, taught me that his memory would live on within me and that I had gained an angel. Tio Milton would always be watching over me. As a young man, the concept of an angel made sense to me, and my grief began to transform. I would even dream about Tio Milton at times and it would give me comfort. His words encouraging me to be responsible lived within me and developed another layer of my character.

We moved several times throughout my elementary school years. I left Magnolia Elementary after the 3rd grade and had attended at least three other elementary schools by 5th grade. Our constant moving was fueled by my stepfather's problem with alcohol. We were evicted several times during my childhood. Instability at home made life at school very challenging for me. I fell behind in my studies and was forced to make new friends every few months. An eviction during my fourth grade even caused me to miss the first half of the school year. Because of all this, I wasn't confident in my academic skills.

I never understood how far behind I was until my Tio Oscar asked his son, Noe, to read out loud to us. My cousin was a year younger than me and was a great reader. Tio Oscar was proud of his son and, as a good father should, encouraged his son to practice his skills. I followed along in the text with my cousin and was overcome with sudden shame. I couldn't understand the very same text he was reading with ease. As his older cousin, I felt inferior.

That embarrassment would follow me into the classroom. Each time Mr. Lampin would call on me to read, I would make an excuse as to why I could not do it. Eventually, he caught on and asked for a parent-teacher conference. With limited English and the help of an interpreter, my mom attended and discovered my areas for growth. While reading was difficult for me, I was good at math. It was one of the few lessons my stepfather taught me as a kid. He would teach me small exercises that honed my ability in math. Being capable in some academic areas emboldened me to practice more often, and soon I began to recognize more words.

The process of learning to read, especially at an older age, was a frustrating one. I was alone most of the time. My mother's limited English and attention to keeping a roof over our heads required I learn to read on my own. Our culture had always prioritized work over school out of necessity. This was a mindset carried from El Salvador and was passed onto me. Overcoming this cultural hurdle added to my focus, determination, and overall grit growing up.

My First Love

I learned all about life with a ball at my feet. — Ronaldinho

My first few years of school were challenging. I hated going to class and being far away from my mother and sisters. Recess during the school day was the only time I forgot about my separation anxiety. That was the time I got to play soccer and all my fears melted away.

Most of my happiest childhood memories centered around a soccer ball at my feet focused on the game. Playing soccer with my cousins Josue and Noe was a rite of passage into our teenage years. Being close in age meant that we grew through our youth together and built a special relationship that we still share almost thirty years later.

A love for soccer was a family legacy for us. A tradition that had been passed down from generation to generation. Conversations at family gatherings and events were centered around the latest win, upset, legendary players, and the history of the game. The sport was our first teacher in important life lessons. Through soccer, we learned what love, passion, and heartache really felt like.

Each day after school, about twenty to thirty kids from the neighborhood would gather to play a game until we were called home for dinner. Even our local gang members would stop to watch us. Josue, Noe, and I would look forward to these afternoon matches and always played on the same team. We were often the youngest kids playing, but we were good, so we always got picked. Our practice together in our free time made us a force to reckon with, despite our smaller stature.

Soccer was always the initial connection I had to new peers in school. It was something consistent for me, despite our constant moving. I was good at it, too, so new kids would eventually welcome me into any game, even if they were hesitant at first. No matter what school I attended, there was always a game after school. Before the final bell rang, the teams had been selected and headed to the pavement field a few blocks away. The game started with a toss of the ball in the air and, for hours, each team would move the ball from one side of the field to the next. It no longer mattered that I was new.

I didn't know it then, but soccer was preparing me with leadership and confidence skills. I was often a team captain and would encourage my peers in our huddles during breaks in the game. I was also chosen to take the final game-winning shots on several occasions. This was either an experience of great joy or pain, depending on whether a goal was scored. I could be the team hero or villain in these situations, and, on more than one occasion, I experienced both. I came home in tears a few times, catching the attention of my stepfather, Carlos.

Carlos and I had very few positive interactions during my childhood, but soccer was something that we were able to bond over. He gave me lessons, teaching me how to handle risk in the high-pressure situations where scoring the winning goal for my team was all on my shoulders. With his introductions to managing fear, I practiced frequently and began to master my mental perseverance. On the field, in those final moments of the game, I was able to handle myself with more and more certainty. Understanding that I had, in fact, been training for this moment, I was prepared. Whether my final shots won the game for us or not, I could walk home with my head held high, knowing I had done my best.

Throughout our elementary school years, my cousins and I would barely beat the sun home for dinner covered in dirt with bloody knees and elbows. Those were our glory days. Those pick-up games gave all of us children freedom from the violence, drug abuse, and poverty so many of our families endured. Joy ruled on the field.

The game deepened my relationship with Tio Oscar as well. Tio Oscar was a man of few words beyond his elaborate storytelling, but he was the closest thing I had to a consistent father figure. The game gave him the opportunity to express love and teach me discipline in ways a conversation never could have done for us. He wasn't a perfect role model. He was, like so many other

Uncle Oscar and his wife Marlene took me to Disneyland for the first time. In this picture are my cousins Josue, Noe and Ana.

men in the neighborhood, a victim of circumstance. He made poor choices in using drugs or looting stores during the riots for extra cash. Tio Oscar, however, wasn't a bad man. He would never punish me harshly. It would be a gentle tug at my ears to quickly correct my behavior. Tio Oscar would bring me along with my cousins to play ball at the local parks, and I enjoyed being included in their excursions outside of the house. Time on the field meant that we would learn, through the game, how to stand our ground if we were confronted by gang members. Tio Oscar used soccer to teach us things that might eventually save our lives.

As kids, we were always hearing stories about the Salvadoran and Honduran national teams during the 1980s. Honoring the team's glory days were the methods our families used to connect us with their home countries we knew so little about. Soccer was a familiar doorway for us as kids to better understand where we came from.

Josue and I after entering Disneyland— Anaheim CA

A decade later, *La Selecta* — the Salvadoran national team — was no longer a competitor in the region. Despite a hefty losing streak, our families would still take us to see El Salvador play at the L.A. Coliseum. We were passionate about our home team and hopeful that they would bring back their winning magic from the '80s. We were often bullied by Mexican American students who ridiculed us each time *El Tri* — a common nickname for the Mexican national team — beat El Salvador. Our community doubled down on our team support. Each time we played our Mexican peers after school, we felt like we were fighting for our family's honor. We dove for balls like we had seen our parent's idols do in the games from the previous decades. Losing wasn't an option.

John Muir Middle School

After jumping from school to school during my elementary school years, my next academic chapter in middle school brought a little more stability. It was the first time in my life where I would be allowed to complete three years of school in the same place. We still moved twice during my 6th-grade year, but it wasn't as bad as the previous five years of school. I would eventually spend most of my time at John Muir Middle School in South Central L.A.

Located less than a mile away from our new home, John Muir Middle School was on the corner of Slauson Boulevard and Vermont Avenue. My family and I knew very little about the school, but our friends from church had never said very good things about it. John Muir was known as a place where drugs and gangs could easily make their way into students' lives. Like every parent with a son or daughter my age, my mother's biggest fear was for me to make decisions that would get me in trouble and lead me down the wrong path. But in our neighborhood, we didn't have many options.

I waited in the main office on my first day of school, the stories from church members running through my head. Administrators were busy gossiping with one another, paying little attention to the fact that both parents and students were in the office. Others were openly chatting about their disappointment that summer was over, and they had to deal with students for another school year. Their lack of enthusiasm to inspire us as young scholars showed with every eye roll in response to processing paperwork and every pop of the gum smacking loudly in their mouths.

When I got into the classroom, most of my teachers asked us to open our books and work from there with little to no instruction. It wasn't uncommon to look up and see our instructors drinking coffee and reading the newspaper. During tests, we would receive hints that we could help each other out if necessary. Teachers were essentially encouraging us to cheat. Even though this was their attempt to make us look better, it was evident that they had little faith in our ability to learn any other way.

Me and some teammates after a Saturday game at John Muir Middle School located near Slauson and Vermont. Soccer was my escape every Saturday morning.

Some of our teachers went above and beyond to help us, and some served as strong role models, supporting us in making important decisions that would welcome new opportunities into our lives. Unfortunately, the bad teachers overshadowed the work the good teachers did every day.

My mother debated transferring me to another school where I would bus out of the neighborhood, but I refused to change schools once again. Middle school brought new challenges with our bodies changing and the gang recruitment pressures getting stronger. Now was not the time to add additional trials of making new friends.

Once the moving slowed down and things became a bit more stable, another looming challenge picked up at this time — gangs. The prime age for young people to get initiated into gangs was eleven to fourteen years old. John Muir was ripe with young soldiers to recruit. Streets were controlled by MS-13 and 18th Street gang members in one part of the city, while the Crips and Bloods ran the other. We were in the center of it all.

Before I made it to middle school, I knew what these fragile years could look like on the other side. My cousins Ernesto and Gilberto were young teenagers when I was growing up. We spent

84

a lot of time together in our early years. As they got older, Ernesto and Gilberto started to spend more time with other young men flirting with the idea of joining a gang. At eleven and twelve years old, my cousins started to cross the line of right and wrong. It started with shoplifting from our local stores.

On one of our walks home from school together, we stopped into a Thrifty Drug Store for snacks. They showed me how to hide candy in my shorts and demanded I follow their lead. I was younger and terrified, but I did what I was told. When I got home, my mother asked how school was and requested I take a bath and get into some clean clothes. I complied as six-year-olds do, with my mind on the Bubble Yum gum and Now and Laters tucked into my elastic waistband. Bathwater running, the candy fell onto the floor. As she looked at me, the knowing disappointment in my mother's eyes made my heart drop and my gut wrench. At first, she was angry and insisted on knowing where the gum and chewies had come from. She knew I had stolen them.

My mother had noticed the changes in my cousins and was already questioning whether or not I should continue spending so much time with them. She liked the idea of having male role models for me in my uncles and older cousins but understood that their choices were starting to make them undesirable mentors. Her anger subsided and she sat me down on the closed lid of the toilet. In the direct and gentle tone, she used to ensure I took in the lesson, my mother explained to me that what I had done was wrong. We talked about choices and discussed how taking things from stores without paying for them could put me in jail. My choices were important and only I could make them for myself.

It wouldn't be long before that lesson would truly sink in. Despite the gangs and drug dealers, the neighborhood had many hardworking mothers and fathers. Like my mother, my aunts and uncles would often work multiple jobs just to make ends meet. For many kids in the early '90s, this meant hanging out in the neighborhood while no one was home. With that environment, it was no surprise that Ernesto and Gilberto weren't my only cousins getting into trouble. One afternoon, we received news that my cousin, also named Moisés, had been shot and killed just a few blocks from our house.

The loss of Moisés was a big one for my family. The police reported it as a gang-related murder and never investigated beyond that to find the person who killed my Tia Martha's son. He was connected to everyone in so many ways. More importantly, I saw how deeply this loss hurt the women in my family. Watching my aunt scream and cry for her son reminded me of the conversation with my own mother in our bathroom after I stole bubble gum and now and later candy from our local drug store.

My choices would always affect other people, for better or for worse. While the person who shot my cousin was to blame for his death, the choices Moisés made put him in that situation. I could not control the actions of others, but I could choose to do better.

Unfortunately, this loss didn't slow my cousins Ernesto and Gilberto down. At this point, they had been arrested for breaking into cars and stealing car stereos and had begun to use drugs and alcohol. Their arrests became more frequent. These young men who were once my best friends drifted further down a path to nowhere, like so many of our neighbors. Even after our cousin's death, they continued to steal and spend time in and out of juvenile detention centers. Eventually, they turned eighteen, and their arrests as adults earned them deportations back to El Salvador. All of the dollars saved, miles walked, and hungry days my uncles and mother sacrificed to bring them into the United States were lost.

Ernesto and Gilberto would make their way back to Los Angeles, only to return to the same streets and life of misconduct. They would both be deported a second time. Again, I thought about choices. The men in my life — my uncles, cousins, and childhood friends — had all made choices that landed them in jail, deported, or killed. I dug into the wisdom of my mother, Abuela Rosa Emília, and my faith. I wanted to be different.

Ingrid

My younger sister, Ingrid, joined me at John Muir when I started 7th grade. She was only a year younger than me, and we spent most of our time together growing up. When I think about my childhood, so many of my memories include my sister Ingrid. I remember helping her learn how to walk and keeping her close to me when we played outside.

As the years went on, however, we slowly started to drift apart. She became more irritable and started to explode with violent outbursts that made it increasingly more difficult to tolerate. Between the existing violence in our home with my stepfather's alcoholism and my challenges with making new friends at school, I couldn't take on the emotional ups and downs of my closest sister.

By the time she started middle school, Ingrid's anger could no longer be contained at home. She initiated fights with both boys and girls in the area, and she often won. Trying to prove their own dominance, older kids would try to bully Ingrid, but she wouldn't allow that and would never back down from a fight. But she was still my little sister, and it was my duty to protect her. I fought countless times on her behalf to defend and protect Ingrid.

Life with our stepfather Carlos and his drunken cycles of abuse were taking a toll on everyone at home, especially Ingrid. She was depressed and angry. As her brother, I witnessed her struggling but never knew how I could support her. When at home, Ingrid started hiding away in her closet and began cutting her wrists. Outside, she continued to get into fights and act out. Things just seemed to spiral downward for my sister in a way that felt so out of control for me.

Ingrid's behavior eventually caught the attention of some of the local kids from both John Muir Middle School and other schools nearby, like Horace Mann Junior High. Many of them were on their way to be initiated into gangs, serving as lookouts when older gang members were selling drugs or robbing neighborhood stores. Just like Ingrid, they were all trying to escape the horror of life at home. They smoked weed, drank, and got in one physical altercation after another. It helped take their mind off the pain and perhaps allowed them to feel something after numbing themselves as a means of self-preservation for such a long time.

One of the girls in the group was named Gina. Gina lived near us and attended Horace Mann Junior High as well. Her mom was addicted to crack cocaine, and she was usually left with little to no supervision at home. Ingrid and Gina became fast friends, and this friendship would be my sister's introduction to drugs and alcohol at just twelve years old. Gina gave Ingrid her first joint, and the pair would soon start smoking marijuana regularly. The more time they spent together, the more space Ingrid had to continue her experimentation with drugs. Carlos, my stepfather, would pass out on the floor, and Ingrid would finish any remaining alcohol he left behind in the bottles near him. Eventually, Ingrid stopped going to her classes. My friends would sometimes tell me that they saw her leaving campus, but no one knew where she went or who she was with.

Ingrid's behavior continued to escalate. She was arrested for the first time at age thirteen for attempting to rob someone at knifepoint. My mother searched the entire neighborhood when Ingrid didn't come home. I went along with her to ask neighbors if they had seen her. We went into local businesses and asked the owners if she had been there. No one had seen Ingrid. We would ultimately learn what happened to her later that evening. This was a process my mother and I would repeat multiple times throughout the years as Ingrid wandered the streets of Los Angeles.

Each time Ingrid came home, she would be more violent and difficult to communicate with. She lashed out on our younger sisters, Karla and Jennifer, slapping them or screaming at them for no apparent reason. As things got worse with Ingrid, my mother would eventually ask her to leave our home. It was no longer safe for the rest of us to have her there. She would spend years bouncing from place to place. She even spent time sleeping on the street, including the infamous L.A. Skid Row.

While my sister deteriorated through her teenage years, I was attending all of my classes, studying, and playing soccer. I avoided the push to smoke weed or drink and never stayed around the gangs long enough for them to push me into joining. While I was sad about my sister and wanted better for her, I was also angry. I eventually distanced myself from the chaos that seemed to surround her. We were taking very different pathways in life, separating us and causing us to drift apart.

Eventually, Ingrid would head back to jail, this time being tried as an adult, after attempting to break into someone's home. At twenty-seven years old, she would take a plea deal of seven years in jail to avoid a loftier sentence of fifteen to twenty years, according to the district attorney. My contact with her was limited during that time as our lives were so drastically different. I would later learn that she likely experienced sexual abuse as a child, a horror that my mother and I would face together with her. Ingrid's healing was something we all took on together. It was something that brought us closer and pushed my mother into making some strong decisions for our family. We grew to understand that the trauma of her childhood had deeply affected and changed Ingrid on an intensely deep level. We know it may take a lifetime for Ingrid to heal as she continues to struggle through life, but we hold onto the faith that one day, we can help her overcome her past.

Fighting To Dream

You are the one. — Mom

While I wasn't getting into regular fights at school like my younger sister Ingrid, violence still lurked around the corner for me. One day, a classmate named Walter, who was much bigger than me, declared to our entire class that he wanted to fight me after school. There was no reason for the fight. I hadn't done anything to him. Walter was friends with local gang members who were pressuring him to prove his manhood. I was an easy target.

Based on height and muscle development, this was a real-life David versus Goliath situation. I was terrified of getting beat up in front of the entire school. I had kept a fairly low profile, only gaining attention on the soccer field. It kept me out of trouble, and I liked it that way. On the day of the scheduled fight, I could barely get through the second period. I was scheming to figure out a way to leave campus without being found. By lunchtime, the fight had turned into a battle of race. Walter was Black and I was Latino. Soon other classmates, many I had never met before, were approaching me and guaranteeing their support in the fight. While I was flattered by their pledge of allegiance, I was still planning my silent escape after the final bell.

When school ended, there were twenty Latino students waiting for me after class. My back-up had arrived, and they escorted me to the basketball courts behind our main campus like a boxer walking into the ring. By the time I reached the courts, I had about 100 Latino students behind me. Walter was also approaching the courts with about the same number of Black students behind him. As usual, we even had older gang members present to take part in after-school activities. Walter and I walked toward each other in the center of the concrete court. We were both asked if we wanted to fight. Walter immediately shouted yes, with his chest puffed out. I didn't want to fight, but I knew I couldn't say this out loud. However, before I even had the opportunity to answer, the crowd shouted, "Heck yea!" That was it. I would fight, and there was no backing down now.

The fight started and I looked up at Walter. He towered over me. I closed my eyes and started throwing punches at the same time Walter did. I connected my first punch, but so did Walter. I fell to the ground with his first hit, and, in a matter of seconds, I had his enormous body standing over me. He threw a barrage of punches to my face and body. At first, I tried to cover myself to block the punches. I could hear my peers shouting and cheering. I worked to control my thoughts and was able to turn my body into a crawl-like position on the ground. Walter was so tall that I could crawl in between his legs. By the time he turned around, I was already standing back up. Walter charged toward me. I fought back as hard as I could by pushing, punching, and kicking him against the fence. It was my turn to regain control of the fight, and the fence gave me the leverage I needed with our height differences.

I couldn't have had Walter against that fence for more than five to ten seconds before a teacher came running over to us to break things up. The other students went running in opposite directions to avoid any punishment. No one had won this brawl, and now we both had to face the consequences with a suspension. As we sat in the office next to each other, we realized how dumb our actions had been. We didn't have to be friends, but we had to respect each other. We were both just trying to make it through school and survive the external pressures of living in an area dominated by gang culture. Neither of us wanted to fight, but it was sometimes the only way of getting the older kids in the neighborhood to leave you alone. Walter had picked a fight with me so that he didn't have to fight the older *vatos* — men — following him home from school.

Walter and I moved on after our brief and very public rumble. I heard that he graduated high school and went on to earn a four-year degree. It made me glad to know that he finished school and that the pressures of the neighborhood didn't break him. I have always wondered if our fight helped him shake the older boys.

Walter wasn't the first time I resorted to violence to handle a conflict. I had plenty of experience of being dragged into fights with my sister Ingrid. Engendered by the prominent gang presence, fighting was a part of the culture in the neighborhood. The boxing ring experience on the basketball courts with Walter was, however, when I made the commitment to myself that I would not fight again. I knew that meant I needed to keep my head down and avoid most social gatherings around school, but I rejected the fear of what might happen to me if I didn't fight back. Fighting didn't make sense to me, so why was I doing it? I felt so disconnected from the inner voice I had grown to rely on. The one that had been built by my Abuela Rosa Emília, my mother, and my strong relationship with God.

Sitting in the office awaiting punishment after being pulled off the courts, I planted new seeds for future dreams. I focused on what I wanted to achieve and the activities that brought me joy. Not surprisingly, my mind and heart wandered back to soccer. I began to reconnect with my inner guide and visualize something bigger. There had to be more to my life than what I was currently sitting in.

A Dream is Born

I knew that becoming a professional soccer player was a long shot for most people. I also knew that my size would likely be a huge barrier to getting into that world. I was reminded of my size all too often, and, despite me still doing well on the field, it was a reality I came to terms with early. Once I had recommitted myself to a larger dream, I observed things in my life that I loved as much as playing the game. I knew that I wanted to remain close to the sport and dreamed of a career where I could interact with the game day to day. I always admired announcers and sportscasters on TV, and that quickly became the dream.

For any soccer enthusiast, there's only one major sporting event that allows you to dream big — the FIFA World Cup. The older you get, the more passionate you become about watching the tournament played every four years. Next to the Olympics, the World Cup is the biggest sporting event on the planet. I was in 7th grade when the World Cup took place in France in 1998. Walking to and from school, I would listen to the games on the radio. I learned the announcer's voices and began to understand their differences in style.

Andrés Cantor, an Argentinian American sportscaster in the '90s, was my favorite. Cantor had emigrated to Southern California as a teen and had just started rising in the mainstream media at that time. I wanted to yell "goooooaaaalllll," like he did, for as long as my lungs would allow. I would practice my "goooooaalll" call walking up and down the railroad tracks on Slauson Avenue, an experience that transported me to the booth above the field where thousands of fans cheered the players on. This became a routine for me, and before I knew it, it became a true calling.

I made it a habit to listen to the radio and simultaneously practice my play-by-play broadcast any chance I got. Without cell phones or YouTube, I would rush back home after school to watch game highlights while counting the days to the weekend when I could watch the full games. As soon as games were over, I would run to the backyard to kick the ball around and practice announcing my own moves. I would put myself up against all the great players of the time — Gabriel Batistuta, Juan Veron, and Ariel "El Burrito" Ortega.

The players and announcers like Andrés Cantor became my mentors. I studied all the tricks of the trade and took notes on how my own style was starting to evolve. While other kids from the neighborhood were gathering after school to hang out, I rarely joined. The commitment I had made to myself to stop fighting was too great to risk. I kept my head down and stayed focused.

Fútbol — soccer — became my religion, and my dedication to studying the game was the main reason why I never joined a gang. The discipline that sports taught me was something that couldn't be learned inside of a classroom. Aside from the rigor of practice in trying to increase my skills to win, soccer was teaching me about teamwork and brotherhood on and off the field. I was learning about the importance of building relationships and how to navigate tricky social situations.

Around the same time, I had sworn off fighting and the other mischievous antics of my peers, I reconnected with an outside league soccer coach, Coach Minor. I had met Coach Minor in the 6th grade but would begin to play for him and the L.A. Inter team at the start of my 7th-grade year. This league was more competitive than the league outside of the normal public-school circuit. Playing in this league would mean more frequent practices and weekend games played on fields around the city. As a kid, I didn't play for many teams, even when I was heavily recruited by the better clubs. My three childhood clubs in Los Angeles were New L.A. Stars, L.A. Inter, and Laguna, where I played along with kids that would eventually become lifetime friends for me.

Coach Minor had worked in the area for years and was well aware of the challenges so many of his students faced. While I wasn't using drugs, I had my own obstacles in making it to practice and games. My mother was often working or occupied at home with my sisters and stepfather, leaving me without a reliable and safe way to make it on time to play.

Coach made an agreement with my mother that he would take responsibility for me during this time, providing my necessary transportation so that I could play. I became one of many players Coach Minor would pick up every Saturday morning to drive to that day's match. I would wake up at 6:00am to walk to our meeting point and wait for Coach Minor to swing by for us around 7:00am. From that car ride forward, we would spend our entire Saturday at some of Los Angeles' and South Central's most popular soccer fields.

We often traveled to *Las Polvosas* — well-known dirt fields located on the corner of 41st and San Pedro Street or off of Compton Avenue. Anyone who played soccer in L.A. during the '90s and early 2000s is familiar with at least one dirt field in the city. With little maintenance required, someone would paint white lines around the field at 6:30am every Saturday before we arrived in preparation for the first game's kick-off an hour later.

We would stay all day at those fields, eight to ten hours at a time, watching teams play and studying their strategies. Time always passed quickly for us; soccer consumed our lives. It was a regular testament to my commitment to myself that I would not allow the threats of my neighborhood to get the best of me. Long Saturdays on the field were always better than long Saturdays of wandering local streets avoiding fights, weed, or booze to pass the time.

We were L.A. Inter, a soccer club formed of different age groups that felt like one big family. Most of my teammates were from humble backgrounds, like myself. Each of us would come ready with change to purchase Mexican food sold by local women on the sidelines. *Sopes, tacos, gorditas, quesadillas* and *aguas frescas* were readily available as early as 9:00am. Heavy, sometimes fried, food was not an ideal meal choice for us as young athletes. But the food was convenient and cheap, both things we needed in order to eat anything on those Saturdays.

We all wore the bright yellow L.A. Inter jersey with pride. It was a replica of the 1990 U.S. World Cup team jersey, complete with three blue stripes on one sleeve. Our team radiated professionalism in those yellow t-shirts. Unlike games in elementary school, each game we played as L.A. Inter was important. The league was competitive, and every goal scored counted toward our ranking. Personally, I felt important and validated with every goal I scored for the team. It felt like I was contributing to something bigger than myself. The league gave me a sense of belonging, a feeling all of us were looking for at the time.

These competitive leagues also weren't free. At the beginning of each year, a fee to play was requested to cover our uniforms and referee fees for every game. As a member of L.A. Inter Club, my mother was required to pay my participation fee, broken down into weekly payments of $10, $5 for the referee fee, and $5 for our uniform.

Things were tight at home with my stepfather's income being sporadic, but my mom always managed to make the payment. She would send me to the field every Saturday with a roll of quarters that amounted to five dollars to cover the referee cost for the day.

It would embarrass me to have to pay with coins, but I appreciated the sacrifices my mother made to give me those five dollars. That money was sometimes needed to do our laundry. My mother's support of soccer was clear with her dedication to finding a way to get me on a team, no matter the financial or logistical challenges.

Playing soccer in South Central Los Angeles wasn't all about the dirt fields but also the camaraderie built during the carpooling. Rides where I made strong connections with kids who were facing similar problems to mine. Young athletes who also used the sport as a vehicle to escape from everything negative that took place in our streets. We sometimes belonged to areas with opposite gangs. Each ride allowed us to share information about what was happening in our own neighborhood. Nonetheless, once we put our jerseys on, we were brothers who would fight for one another on the field.

Coach Minor had a big truck with a camper in the back that he would use to transport me and my ten to eleven L.A. Inter teammates. We would lay down in the back of the truck camper to avoid being pulled over by the police. While this was extremely dangerous and risky, Coach Minor and many of our parents allowed it, knowing that the risk of staying in the neighborhood could be much worse.

These rides, so closely squished together in the back of the truck, built unavoidable bonds between us. Coach Minor's son, Raymond, was on the team, along with his niece Roxana and nephew Marvin, who became one of my best friends. Other friends of mine from John Muir Middle School also played for L.A. Inter, including Bobby and José, also known as "Shorty."

These were chaotic times for us kids growing up in South Central Los Angeles. We were preparing to transition to high school and were confronted daily with tough decisions that would define our lives well beyond the moment. Our group of twelve slowly dwindled down to four or five players showing up for Saturday games at *Las Polvosas*. On many occasions, Coach Minor would knock on doors to plead with players to rejoin the team.

For those of us who played with L.A. Inter until the end, we now realize that those rides in the back of that truck probably saved our lives. Coach Minor had dedicated his time through soccer to make a difference in our lives and the greater community. He did something not many have the courage to do. Coach Minor gave us something to work for outside of our reality. He gave us experiences and taught us discipline that we look back on with endless gratitude.

PART 2
Starting My Journey

Middle school graduation also marked the beginning of the end of my mother's relationship with Carlos. The summer between 8th and 9th grade was one of the craziest time periods in my life. I used to believe that my parents would find a way to work things out solely based on our faith. If they couldn't see the way, I prayed that God himself would show them. If not for them, for the seven of us who were strongly affected by it all. Instead, my prayers would not be answered, and I would be forced to once again grow up a little more. The older I got, the more conscious I became of our financial problems. I was the one often sent to our neighbors to ask for a cup of sugar or a box of cereal we would later pay back. I sometimes took it upon myself to walk a few blocks to sell whatever aluminum cans and plastic containers I might be able to collect in exchange for a few dollars. Money we would simply use to get away for a few hours.

I wanted to keep my younger siblings as far away from all the drama that surrounded our home at times by distracting them with daily activities. The summer before I entered high school, my sisters and I swam at the public pool near our house almost every day with the other kids from our neighborhood. For about 75¢ each, we were able to pay the entry fee to get out of the house and enjoy a few laughs with neighborhood kids. Van Ness Park on Slauson Blvd was our favorite place to be every year from June to August. Summer programs for low-income families like ours provided us with a daily lunch before going swimming. When we got back home, it was back to facing our reality, which was at an all-time low.

By 1999, my parents had been divorced for three years. Although, that wouldn't stop Carlos from coming back home as he pleased. He acted as if the separation had never taken place. Afraid to tell him to leave, my mother pretended to be okay with his return. As kids, we had heard the stories of hardship my aunts and uncles had endured growing up. I never imagined that my siblings and I would have our own experience in Los Angeles. As welfare dependents, any mistake in paperwork could lead us into a downward financial spiral for months. Government checks were the only reason we were able to get by when my mother wasn't able to work. That summer, I learned what real inner strength meant through the difficult times my family would endure. More importantly, those hard moments fortified my relationship with my mother and siblings. We would learn to depend on each other like never before.

When bills could no longer be paid, things would take a drastic turn at home. We would lose basic utilities like electricity, running water, and gas. Bills were just the tip of the iceberg of our problems. Distress would follow us during the next couple of years, but we weren't the only ones. The red house to our left was already empty and going through a foreclosure. The previous tenants had been evicted months before. The white paper with big red letters was still there as proof. The house to our right was owned by an LAPD detective that mostly kept to herself. We would only see her when she left for work early in the morning. Meanwhile, our problems of having no running water would force us to do something unthinkable.

For reasons unknown, the empty red house next door still had running water. Without thinking twice, we would connect a water hose near the back of the house in order to take water for ourselves. Old enough to know what we were doing was wrong but necessary to survive, we began by only taking a few gallons to drink every day. Soon enough, it became the water we used for everything, including taking cold showers during the hot summer. Initially, the plan was for the house next door to get us by for a couple of days. This would buy my mother time to figure out how to get us back to normal since Carlos couldn't be depended on.

When we learned we wouldn't be able to pay our debt, the red house next door became vital to our day-to-day living. I pretended that things were okay, although deep down, I knew things were only getting worse. No one in our neighborhood had a clue about what was happening, and if they did, they kept it to themselves. It felt as if a volcano was ready to erupt, and my family was only feet away from the blast. Embarrassed to tell any of our family members or friends, it remained our secret.

The idea of surviving at whatever cost was something my mother knew firsthand. She wasn't new to experiencing hardship like this. But we were. This led her to talk to us whenever we found ourselves alone with her. Moments in which she would tell us that things wouldn't always be this way. She wanted us to have faith that things would improve, and we had to stick together. Reminding me personally that I had to be strong for my younger sisters who needed me to be their example.

That also meant playing along with whatever plan Carlos came up with in order to get us through the day. His first idea was to climb an enormous avocado tree behind the red house. A decision that went against keeping a low profile and not attracting too much attention from the neighbors. Every morning after our neighbors headed to work, I headed up the tree with Carlos to cut avocados. After we filled a few baskets, we would wrap them around newspaper and store them until they were ripe. Climbing up any type of tree for food was mostly something practiced in Central America. I didn't agree with the action but knew it also meant we would have something else to eat aside from the lunches we received at the park. I would choose to see our experience as proof of how resilient my family has always been, regardless of the circumstances.

Our backyard became a garden for several months where we had grown "*guisquiles*," also known as christophine or chayote. It was an edible plant within the gourd family, very similar to a firm squash. *Guisquiles* grew quickly, which made it easier to add to our daily meals. It was also true we were walking over eggshells, and I lived with the fear that the seven of us could be removed by child services at any given moment. The more time I had to look around and understand my surroundings, the less I wanted to be a part of it. My dreams were different. I wanted to conquer the world and head to places I saw on television.

I had dreams of traveling abroad to play competitive soccer against teams from different countries. I imagined myself learning about different cultures and coming back home with amazing stories to tell my teachers and friends. But it was hard to believe that would ever be possible in those times. As an alternative, I would have to be okay with just listening to my classmates' stories. Many of them, like me, had also been born in the U.S. but would travel back to Central America with their families during the holidays. Since I didn't have that experience, I had to vicariously live through them. It was becoming clear to me then that I would have to work twice as hard to change my future. Without an education or a stable job, it was nearly impossible for my mother to take care of us all.

Summer vacation was anything but a vacation that year. The three-month break became a clear picture of what society believed my fate would be. My neighborhood was the perfect example of what awaited me if I didn't act soon. Our unstable living conditions that summer brought my stepfather to carry out one of the most dangerous and stupidest things I've ever seen a person do.

After living in the dark for about a week with no electricity and only candles as lights, Carlos climbed up the electric post next to our house to illegally bring electricity into our home. Doing so by connecting a few wires and hooking a power cord to the post. It was like placing a band-aid over a wound that needed stitches.

We took advantage of the unpaid services for about two months, even creating a system to prevent us from getting caught. Whenever we would see someone from the Department of Water and Power working nearby, we would disconnect everything. I would convince my sisters to play a game to see who spotted the DWP worker first. This helped distract my siblings from what was really going on at home. My stepfather never talked about our situation or attempted to explain things to any of us. This only made me lose respect for him as a man. I would stop calling him dad and address him as Carlos from that point forward. It was my way of getting him back. I knew it hurt him because he loved me like a son in his own way.

One late night, Carlos' invention backfired when a DWP crew showed up at our house without warning. My sisters and I were all in front of the television when we heard a knock on the door.

My mom whispered to turn the TV off and asked everyone to be quiet. She had no idea who was knocking at that time of night and thought silence might keep us out of trouble.

My mother opened the door to reveal two DWP workers. She had forgotten that the electricity cables we used were still connected outside. My stepfather ran to disconnect the cables, but it was too late. Workers had already spotted the wiring, and our free electricity source was discovered. At first, the workers were angry at how dangerously close the cables were to blowing a transformer and leaving the entire block without electricity. Or even worse, electrocuting someone. Minutes after carefully observing it, they whispered amongst themselves how creative people could be when in need. The workers walked along the side of the house and peered through the windows at me and my sisters. I made eye contact with one of them and saw a look of sympathy returned. When being asked if they understood how dangerous our unconventional electrical hook-up had been, my parents looked down in shame. Neither my mother nor Carlos responded. The DWP workers disconnected our flimsy connection to the post outside and warned Carlos against doing something similar again before they left.

My stepfather, Carlos, was always a proud man. That evening, his body language exuded embarrassment. He didn't have to say a word for us to understand how absolutely defeated he felt. In a way, this made me feel even more resentful towards him. I loved him because he was the closest thing to a father I had ever known; however, I was of the age to understand that his electrical connection could have resulted in the workers calling child services on my mother. His inability to provide our basic needs, like light and water, could have resulted in my siblings and me being ripped away from our mother.

Just a few days later, we returned home from the park with the lights and water back on in our house. This time, getting electricity into our home the legal way. My mother called this a miracle, as we had an outstanding debt of over $2,000 that neither parent could pay. Years later, I would learn that it was, in fact, my mother who borrowed the money from a family friend to get our lights back on. Once again, my mother was able to provide for us no matter the circumstance.

By the end of the summer, I had realized a few things about myself that would change the way I approached the next chapter in my life. The first thing was my strong determination to reject anything negative anyone said about my family. Beginning with the idea that I was incapable of finishing school based on my family's past educational failures. The summer of '99 taught me that I could overcome a great deal of adversity. It was the year when I understood that education was vital in whatever successful path I chose to follow. Education was one of the main reasons my entire family struggled to do better than hard labor work. I would change the mental picture I had of myself that was filled with obstacles and dead ends. Replacing it with a picture of me walking across the stage to receive a high school diploma four years later. I had no idea how I would accomplish my goal. I just knew that it wouldn't happen unless I took the first step forward.

Welcome to Los Angeles High School

Do what is easy and your life will be hard, do what is hard and your life will be easy — Les Brown

By the time I was heading to high school, my voice and body weren't the only things changing. I had serious goals. Many of my friends from John Muir and L.A. Inter were applying to attend Manual Arts High School, the high school with all the best soccer players. The idea of playing on a super team excited everyone.

I attended Crenshaw High School for just one week before deciding to transfer. It only took a few days to realize how dangerous the school was. On the first day of school, another freshman, new to high school just like me, was beaten up during lunch for wearing a red shirt. We were in Crip territory and the only color allowed around them was blue. The same student was jumped by Crips after school a few days later. I had seen enough. The fights and bullying within my first five days were enough to want out. I wanted a fresh start where the colors I wore wouldn't get me into trouble or confused with belonging to a gang. While I still lived in the neighborhood, my future wasn't there.

At church, the other kids my age went to Los Angeles High School. They shared a diverse array of experiences with me during the youth group I attended every Saturday. I had known many of them since I was young. Attending church, no matter how chaotic times got at home, was always consistent for us. Listening to trusted friends that were also guided by strong faith, it didn't take much to convince me that I needed to transfer to Los Angeles High School. I just wanted to escape the day-to-day violence in the hall and make the soccer team.

I begged my mother to transfer me to L.A. High where I would be safer. After pleading my case, she accepted, and we used my distant uncle's address in order for me to get in. Uncle Alex had married into the family and went to our same church. He knew how difficult the high school climate could be and gladly allowed us to use his address to bring me into the district. Uncle Alex did this, however, with the stipulation that I was to keep good grades and stay away from trouble. If that agreement was broken, I would no longer be able to use the address.

Los Angeles High School wasn't the prettiest school I had ever seen. On the contrary, it looked like a jail from the outside, but once you stepped inside, there was a whole energy about the place. I was now entering a new world, one that I knew little about. The little I knew about the high school experience came from the family members who had made it there but had failed to finish. Their stories usually included comments that school sucked and the teachers were tough for no reason. So many of my family members had resorted to blaming others instead of working hard to complete their education. It was an unfortunate side effect of an educational system that showed no faith in the ability of its students.

Inside campus at L.A. High, the first thing you notice is the giant L.A. High Romans mural on the side of the school gym. The diverse student body walked around, proud to be a Roman. Latinos still made up a majority of the population, with African American students making up the next largest group. However, the Asian students stood out the most for me. It was the first time in my life I was attending school with other ethnicities that were not Latino or Black. This meant that L.A. High offered classes not normally found in other schools, such as Korean studies and language. Our campus reflected the diversity of the city of Los Angeles.

Academically, school was much harder for me than I had anticipated before my transfer. I started to lag behind in some of my classes. All of those semesters in middle school where I skirted by, passing without learning much, were now compounded and catching up with me. I had very little guidance and no one to hold me accountable. While my friends from church went to Los Angeles High School, I rarely saw them amongst the hundreds of other students on campus. I roamed through the first few months of high school without much direction.

105

I did not hang out with any particular group. Instead, I walked around observing the different groups around campus. We had gifted smart kids that were studying during break times as well as students who only went to school because their parents forced them to. The rockers and school band members hung out in the "quad." Our band was the most underrated group of students in the entire school, with ten consecutive city championships to prove it. On the other end of campus, there was "the spot." Kids wearing brand names and the latest sneakers were the only group allowed to hang out in the area.

My first semester, while I didn't belong to any particular group, I did spend much more of the time trying to fit in with the cool kids at the spot. They all wore the latest fashions, from Sean John to Rocawear. Jordan sneakers and Timberland boots were the preferred footwear of almost every student hanging around the spot. The cool kids never seemed to need anything. They always had money for lunch and snacks. Some even had cell phones, which at the time was unheard of for high school students. They would cut class often and, eager to please them, I would join them. Working to hang out with them consumed my time and most of my mental space, which left very little time to finish my schoolwork.

After a semester of chasing acceptance and popularity, I received the worst report card I have ever received in my entire life. I completed my first semester of high school with A's in history, Korean studies, and physical education and F's in science, math, and English. I didn't even realize it was possible to get an F. I had always felt that you needed to try to do so poorly. How could I allow myself to do that?

The consequences of such a report card also meant that I could no longer play soccer. There was a minimum grade point average all students were required to hold in order to play. I was no longer eligible, having let my GPA fall so low. Second semester, I would have to watch the soccer team from the bleachers. I was devastated.

Being forced to sit and watch my teammates play from the sidelines would allow me to think and put things into perspective for me that second semester. Nothing was more painful than not being able to play the sport that I loved. Over the last few months of my freshman year, I had the time to reflect on my choices and how those had led me to sitting on the sidelines. I thought back to other choices I had made with my cousins and other kids from the neighborhood. I had chosen to keep my head down and stay focused on my sports goals rather than steal from corner stores and hang out with local gangs. I was once again faced with another choice to make for my high school career and experience.

Soccer wasn't my only problem at the end of my freshman year. I had made a promise to Uncle Alex that I would do my best to get good grades in exchange for the use of his address. The three F's I had received were enough reason for Uncle Alex to end our agreement and send me straight back to Crenshaw High. My choices could potentially send me back to the place that had me constantly looking over my shoulder in fear of violence. My choices could bring me to a place that didn't have a real soccer team. A place with no potential for activities beyond violence.

The initial stumble of my high school career did more than just keep me off the soccer field. It was another wake-up call. My day-to-day routines were connected with larger outcomes in my life. If I wanted to stay on the team, I had to put the daily work into attending classes and finishing my homework. The bad news of my first semester deepened my connection to myself, my inner voice, and my life vision. It helped me understand my goals better and what was required of me to achieve those goals.

Making amends with Uncle Alex, I convinced my family that I had learned my lesson and would quickly improve my grades. With grace, my uncle gave me another chance. I was determined to make it back on the team and I began to take things seriously. I attended all my classes and studied every chance I got. Like so many other occasions, soccer became the reason to do well in school. It pushed me to improve my habits to catch up in order to be on the field. It was another moment of clarity that soccer was my compass and had not failed in showing me the right way to go.

With my mind refocused on school and soccer, I started my second semester in search of teachers that genuinely cared about us as students and our capacity to learn. Similar to middle school, there were good and bad teachers at L.A. High School. The bad teachers held the same disinterest in the students, and some even assumed we were all gang bangers and criminals. The good teachers, however, were the ones that could push you to be the best version of yourself. They required consistent effort and left an everlasting impression with difficult questions for us to ponder about what we wanted from our lives.

Mr. Edwards was one of L.A. High School's English teachers. His style of teaching was unorthodox and highly criticized around the school by some of his peers. He spoke his mind about anything and everything, even if it offended the other teachers. I took Mr. Edwards' class my first semester when I was still finding my way and lacked a general direction. In true Mr. Edwards form, he told me I was a lazy student and concluded my fall by giving me one of my first F's.

When I returned to freshman year for the spring semester, my focus had changed, and I knew I needed Mr. Edwards' direct style to help guide me back to the soccer field. He would tell me I would not make it to college if I continued on the path I had flirted with my first semester. Most of my family and neighborhood had never completed high school. No one on my block talked about college, and most adults working in my area held jobs that required little to no education. College wasn't on my radar.

I was eager to return to Edwards' classroom for the second semester because I respected his opinion. I knew I could trust his guidance. Not only was I hoping for a role model, but Mr. Edwards was fun. He loved rap music and sports just as much as we did. We could chat with him about popular culture easily. He always seemed to support any creative ideas we might have, no matter how crazy they seemed, as long as they would keep us out of trouble.

Every day, before Mr. Edwards started his class, we all took ten minutes to meditate about life. This was an exercise I was unfamiliar with, especially in school. The closest thing I had ever done was praying at our Christian church. At first, the practice of silence in school seemed odd, but, with my new focus, it allowed me to visualize the soccer field and prepare for the lesson ahead. It was a leveling space to get ready to learn.

Mr. Edwards also spoke about college and university often. He would allow us to ask questions about what life on campus might be like, what we could learn about, and, most importantly, how to get there. Mr. Edwards was the first person to introduce me to the idea of going to college. He had planted a seed of possibility within me that we regularly nurtured together in class as we discussed how I could get there. This idea pushed me to keep expanding my horizons and dream about things beyond what I saw on a day-to-day basis.

We kept journals in Mr. Edwards' class as well, and he gave us an opportunity to write in them every day. I often wrote about soccer, especially my hopes of getting back on the field soon. We would even read our entries out loud to the class sometimes, which built my confidence in speaking in front of crowds. With more conversations about college, however, I started to connect my aspirations of working in sports to college. My dream of becoming a sports announcer could become a reality with additional training in college. Without knowing it, Mr. Edwards' class reset my vision back onto something I had started in middle school, my future career.

By the end of my second semester, I had turned an F grade to a B+. I didn't know it then, but Mr. Edwards had become the teacher and mentor I had been looking for. His class exercises helped to push me beyond what I thought was possible. Mr. Edwards helped me regain my direction. He became an important male figure for me as well, something I desperately lacked at home.

Señora Gibbs

Mrs. Gibbs was one of the most hated teachers at L.A. High. She was strict and based her classroom around discipline and great behavior. She reminded me of the mean teachers my uncles and aunts talked about having when they were kids. Being tardy was not tolerated in Mrs. Gibbs' classroom, and it would cost you an hour of standing up for the entire lesson that day.

Mrs. Gibbs taught Spanish, a subject that I felt I could pass with little effort since Spanish was my first language and always spoken in my home. This was an attitude I realized I quickly needed to adjust. While I spoke the language, there were grammatical nuances I still needed to learn. In addition, and more importantly, Mrs. Gibbs' structure taught me discipline that I seriously needed.

As I fought off the urge to skip class and hang out with the kids in their Jordans and FUBU, I began to abide by Mrs. Gibbs' rules and show up in the way she demanded. My mother taught me discipline at home, but that was things like taking out the trash when asked and helping out around the house with chores. Mrs. Gibbs challenged me with discipline in a different manner. She required us to have self-discipline and to be responsible for regulating our own actions and behaviors. I was responsible for managing my time to maintain punctuality. Mrs. Gibbs taught me discipline and responsibility through consequences to my actions, instead of being told what to do all the time.

Following the rules permitted a closer relationship with Mrs. Gibbs. She would ask me to stay after class for a few minutes just to check in and chat about my studies and home life. Our conversations became a daily routine, and with my newfound appreciation for the Spanish language, I strove to become the best student I could be. I got hyper-focused on perfecting my writing and reading in my family's native language. The pride in my studies helped renew a sense of respect and joy in my culture.

Mrs. Gibbs would also introduce me to advanced classes known as "AP" courses. Mrs. Gibbs, much like Mr. Edwards, wanted to see me excel beyond high school and go to college. AP courses were a way to get to college and obtain credits more quickly and affordably. I was unsure about taking more difficult classes. I was still a bit insecure about my poor report card in the first semester and felt like I was still catching up. All of the students in the AP courses had almost perfect grades, and they seemed so much smarter than me. However, I had nothing to lose and everything to gain, and I gave in to Mrs. Gibbs' encouragement. My competitive nature pushed me to achieve what my peers were able to achieve. If they could do it, I could too.

When our AP semester began, I was the odd man in the classroom. Most of the students in class had studied together for years and I was the newcomer who didn't know anyone. Motivated to meet my new goals, I came to class early every day with a laser focus on excelling, just like my peers. If I worked hard enough, I knew I could do it. Mrs. Gibbs would often call my name to get me out of my comfort zone. After a few weeks of me showing up each day for class and working hard, my peers started to encourage me as well. The intimate support of my AP Spanish course gave me the courage to endeavor further in my academic goals. While soccer remained a primary focus for me, I was gaining new confidence in myself as a student, and that new sense of determination helped me keep moving when things got hard.

Mrs. Gibbs and I bonded on a personal level that extended outside of the classroom. She would hire me to put up her Christmas lights for several years. She would pick me up and drive me to her house to hang the lights or do other odd jobs around the house.

One day after school, we headed to her place for me to move boxes and help her organize her garage. As soon as we pulled into the driveway, Mrs. Gibbs mentioned that something was wrong and out of place. She looked closely at the house and quickly realized someone had broken into her home. I told her to take a deep breath and to sit with me on the curb while we called the police and waited for them to arrive.

Shortly after our call, police arrived on scene, and cautiously entered the house to begin investigating. Once the house had been cleared and the police communicated further with officers at the station, they concluded that her home had not been burglarized. Instead, Mrs. Gibbs' home had been broken into by special detectives in pursuit of a man who had led the police on a car chase and was on the run. They had broken in without permission and had not yet had the chance to notify her properly.

Mrs. Gibbs was terrified by the idea that there was a potentially violent man running from the police in her neighborhood and almost fainted when she heard the news. I stood with her during the conversation with the police and reminded her to breathe. I helped calm her down to the point where police could leave and helped her back inside. That experience together strengthened our bond and created a more familial relationship between us. Mrs. Gibbs was becoming an aunt unlike any I had ever had. An aunt that appreciated academic achievement and one far away from the harsh realities of violence and poverty.

Both Mrs. Gibbs and Mr. Edwards made sure to keep an eye on me throughout my four years of high school, independent of whether or not I was in their class. They went the extra mile to make sure I stayed on the right track for a brighter future. They helped me find the courage and determination to do things I never knew were possible. Things I had never even considered. They created a safe and caring space for me to go when things were unstable at home. I was not alone either. Mrs. Gibbs and Mr. Edwards impacted dozens of students who still remember the ways in which their teaching styles and extra care changed their life trajectories. My relationships with those teachers significantly changed the course of my journey.

Saved by Welfare

In my first three years of high school, as with all my childhood, we continued to receive government assistance through welfare, which provided some stability at home. We would add rice and eggs to cheap ramen noodles to keep the food stretching far enough for all of us to eat. When more money was available from my mom's sporadic work, we would buy cheese and tortillas for homemade quesadillas.

My mother was a single mother about ninety percent of the time, which is what helped qualify us for the program. We were required to make monthly visits to an office where my siblings and I would speak to a program officer.

As a teenager, these monthly visits were the most humiliating things we could endure. We called the welfare "the W" to avoid being ridiculed by friends and neighbors. In school, receiving welfare was looked down upon, even though a large percentage of students at L.A. High were in the same situation. Each time we stepped into the building I would look around to see if I knew anyone sitting in the waiting room. On more than one occasion, I ran into a classmate or someone from my neighborhood. It was awkward and, more often than not, we would pretend not to see each other.

Being on welfare could result in a high possibility that you would be bullied by other kids. The students hanging at the spot with their Sean Jean hoodies and Timberland boots were typically the ones teasing others for being poor, and when they said something, everyone listened. No matter what other kids said, however, we truly needed the help. We would not have survived without that monthly check to pay rent and the food stamps to feed all eight of us. Even with assistance, we were barely scraping by and lived check to check. As an undocumented immigrant, my mother's work was never stable or guaranteed.

For years, as the eldest, I was responsible for making our weekly visits to the grocery store. My mom had prepared me to do this since I was in elementary school. We would go together, and she would show me how to choose the produce in the market as we went aisle by aisle looking at different things we usually bought.

Feeding seven kids wasn't a simple task, especially on a bare-bones budget. My mother would get creative with her expertise in the kitchen. She taught us that we could adapt under any circumstance, and we always held our faith. Every dinner was accompanied by a prayer of gratitude. We would often hear stories of my mother growing up in El Salvador and her prayers for a better life. She would remind us that the family worked hard for us to be here and that things would continue to get better.

Based on my mother's stories, my siblings and I all concluded that it was better to be poor in the United States than in my family's country of origin, El Salvador. In the U.S., I still had the opportunity to complete school and work towards goals I had set for myself. In El Salvador, a young man my age would likely already be working full-time to provide for his family. Very rarely did young people without means have the liberty to make goals for themselves in Central America.

At the "W" office, when I could feel myself getting embarrassed, I reminded myself of what a blessing having access to such assistance was for my family. I thought about the opportunity to finish high school being right in front of me, something my mother was never able to do. I was able to dream and set goals for myself. When my mother and uncles weren't much older than I was, they had no other option than to risk their lives to avoid the danger around them. With gratitude, I focused on the freedom in front of me and chose not to allow us being on welfare to daunt me. Instead of an excuse or a distraction, I would use welfare as a motivator to keep working hard.

My last two years of high school were met with a considerable amount of chaos at home. The motivation I had gained from reflection at the "W" prepared me for what was to come next. In the middle of my 10th-grade year, we were evicted from the home we had stayed in for years. As I had grown accustomed to doing, I looked to God and prayed for guidance and stability. I vowed to stay committed to my goals of finishing high school.

For the first few weeks after our eviction, my sisters went to an aunt's house and I stayed with my friend Marvin while my mother looked for a place to live. Marvin lived around the corner from us, and we had grown up playing soccer together. Eventually, I would go to stay with my Tia Yesenia for another two weeks until my mother found a new place where we could all be reunited.

After a few weeks of searching, we moved into my Tia Janet's studio apartment inside an old two-story building closer to L.A. High, near the corner of Washington Blvd and Vermont Avenue. Only meant to accommodate one to two people, the apartment was extremely small for all nine of us — my five sisters, younger brother and myself, my mother, and Tia Janet. Tia Janet moved all the furniture out of the apartment to make more space for everyone. We all slept on the carpet each night on top of and under multiple layers of blankets and pillows.

Before bed, we would pray and thank God for providing a roof over our heads. I would often add my own silent prayer, asking for strength and wisdom to overcome the tough times. As a family of eight, we had been transferred from a three-bedroom duplex to my aunt's apartment that was smaller than our old living room. As teenagers, high school was already hard enough to assimilate to, and this added an extra layer of stress for us.

I worked hard to find my own stability and created a new routine. I left for school early every day to finish my homework in the morning to get out of the way at home and to free up my afternoons for soccer practice. It was easier to get up earlier to finish homework than it was studying in the closet or bathroom of our cramped apartment.

Towards the end of my 11th grade year of high school, LAUSD bought the land under our apartment building to build a new high school. This would mean that we would need to move once again. Even with a couple of months to prepare, my mother still wasn't able to find another place that we could afford. We also could not find a family member or friend to take all eight of us into their homes. Most of our close relatives had large families of their own and were also working hard to make ends meet.

My mother, along with four of my sisters, went to a shelter near Venice Beach. My sister Joana and younger brother Abraham went to stay with my Tio Oscar, and I went to live with my Tia Yesenia, or Tia Yessie as I called her, on Leeward Avenue near McArthur Park. The area was just a few minutes away from downtown Los Angeles, close enough to see the tall buildings. The neighborhood, however, was more dangerous than any of the other places my family had lived in the past.

Along with the familiar patterns of gang violence, Leeward Avenue held a whole new level of hostility. Dead bodies were commonly found lying in alleyways and in the trunks of parked cars along the main road. We saw a dead body once with our own eyes. Death seemed to be all around us most days on Leeward Avenue. Arrests were rarely made, and the police force seemed to be non-existent in the neighborhood. Officers were generally unkind to Leeward residents, assuming that everyone was a gang member, and that violence would continue no matter what they did. This left a giant vacuum for local gangs to roam freely. I would walk to school every morning with Tia Yessie's daughter, my younger cousin Loana, to keep her safe and in an attempt to ward off any gang bangers with motives for bullying. This rarely worked, and we would often run most of the way there.

That year, I got my first official job working for the owner of one of the soccer teams I played for. He owned a security company, and I would help him with installations and maintenance during my breaks from school. During my vacations, I would earn up to $250 per week. I finally had a small pot of money to spend on myself. I purchased the clothes we could never afford and that I always admired of the kids that hung out at the spot on campus. I bought myself a silver chain, a nice pair of Nike Air Jordan 1's, and eventually a Nextel phone with a fancy belt carrier to hold it.

It wasn't long after I strapped my new mobile phone to my waist that I gained more attention from local gang members looking for trouble. I looked like I had money; I had made sure of that, and now the Leeward *cholos* wanted a chunk of my money for themselves. One day, departing from the bus after school, I noticed a man sitting on a bike at the bus stop. After a few steps in the direction of home, I noticed I was being followed. My heart started beating faster and the sixth sense I had developed from being raised in bad neighborhoods kicked in. I slowly hid my chain and phone in a small pocket of a backpack that I wore across my chest, along with the $250 I was carrying around.

Bike man continued to follow me for several blocks further along my route home. I realized he wasn't going anywhere. I had several choices. I could run the rest of the way back to my aunt's apartment. I could turn around, confront the man, and fight my way out like I had done before in school. Logic told me to avoid fighting. I had no idea whether the man was armed with a knife or a gun. I decided to throw an obstacle into his path. I called Tia Yessie when I was only a few blocks away and continued my walk home.

Tia Yessie left her building and started walking toward me, ready to meet me at the halfway point in the middle of the street. When we met, Tia Yessie grabbed my shoulders and pushed me toward her apartment. She told me to go inside and to do it quickly. With my back turned, I heard Tia Yessie yell to the man to go home and to leave us alone. At first, he looked back at her defiantly, with no intention of turning around. Looking up to see me peeking at the stand-off unfolding on the street, he lifted both hands up as if to say, "I surrender." He turned around and rode his bike in the opposite direction.

Returning to the house, my Tia Yessie asked me to sit down with her in the kitchen. She had lived on Leeward Avenue for a long time and had seen too many young men lose their lives. She explained to me that while tonight we had both avoided tragedies, she would not always be able to protect me. Tia Yessie was respected in the neighborhood and was friends with many of the *cholo*'s mothers in the area. The boys respected my aunt, as well as other elders in the neighborhood, when it suited them. However, business would always reside over respect, and we only "won" that night because the man on the bike was alone.

117

My aunt told me that she loved me too much to lose me. She told me that she was proud of what I was doing in school, with my new job, and with soccer. Tia Yessie and I agreed that I had too much to lose to stay in Leeward any longer. I thanked her and called my friend Marvin, once again, to see if there was space for me at his house to finish high school. Marvin agreed, and I packed my things that evening.

Two days later, a teenage boy walking down my Tia Yessie's street refused to give up his belongings to a few *cholos* and was shot dead. The details of the shooting were fuzzy, and it didn't attract much attention from local media or authorities. He was just another young man shot in a sea of dozens. He was a high school student, just like me. My Tia Yessie called me crying, and we both prayed over the phone for God's protection over us that evening. From what we had heard, the events of that poor kid's death were frighteningly similar to the events of the afternoon she saved me from the bike man. With gratitude, I continued the beginning of my senior year homeless yet alive.

My final stretch of high school was in front of me. However, I was having trouble feeling the same excitement that many of my peers seemed to feel. Despite my gratitude to Marvin and his family for taking me in, the embarrassment pressed on me. I was still making up credits for how far I had fallen behind from middle school and failing my first semester. So, I had decided it was best to quit my job to dedicate more time studying for the additional credits I needed to qualify for college.

I started to feel out of place. Many of my peers had already decided to move straight into the workforce upon graduation. Finishing school was not a priority for my family, and I found that expectations for me among my relatives were fairly low. My aunts and uncles had mostly dropped out long before they reached this point in school, not because they were incapable, but because they needed to work to support the greater family. In general, not many kids did much to move out of the neighborhood. It was only when sports were involved did kids like me leave the area. There was little inspiration around me, and I felt rather alone.

This feeling of isolation was deepened by the distance from my siblings and mother. Instead of senior year trips to Venice Beach, I would spend my weekends traveling to see my mother and sisters at the shelter. Although these visits were important too, as I needed this time with my family, they also reminded me of how little I could do for them. Adding guilt to the long list of worries I was carrying. The pressure quickly started affecting my performance at school.

One Saturday afternoon, I was visiting my mother as usual. She could see the stress weighing on me. With a stern look, she urged me to tell her what was wrong. I gave in and explained how mentally drained I had felt. My lack of energy and living situation had caused me to fall behind in my schoolwork again, and I wasn't sure I would be able to graduate.

With tears in her eyes, my mother guided me away from the group of Marvin and my siblings. She reminded me of how difficult her journey to Los Angeles had been, but that it was worth it because I had the opportunity to graduate high school. My mother told me that she knew I would be the one to create a new legacy for our family. This wasn't a demand but rather an assurance of her faith in me and my capabilities. Quitting was not an option.

I was moved by the firm yet loving direction my mother had given me. My mother, aunts, and uncles had told me they were proud of me before. However, that was different than being charged with leading our family into a new future. While some would see my mother's confession as an added burden, I found a renewed sense of confidence. My doubts had dispersed, knowing I had the faith of my family behind me.

I fell back on my own faith. I said daily affirmations and prayers to keep my faith and remind myself that I had everything I needed to achieve my wildest dreams. I held gratitude close and was comforted in knowing that all my hardships had a purpose. I was born with the strength of my family. I was not born to fail.

Be Honest

With graduation only a few weeks away, I prepared myself to receive another poor grade on a paper I had recently written for my English class with Mr. Feinstein. While I had been focused most of the semester, I had been struggling with being so far away from family, especially my younger siblings, at the time I was writing the paper. I had little privacy to focus at Marvin's, and I had made a few extra visits to my mother during the week that had taken me away from the time I needed to write an appropriate paper. This grade was the only thing standing between me and my cap and gown.

Determined to walk across the stage with everyone else, I had no other choice but to speak honestly with Mr. Feinstein. I had not developed the strongest relationship with him thus far and was not looking forward to sharing the details of my family's current living situation. But I needed another chance to write the paper.

Mr. Feinstein was one of the most respected teachers in all of Los Angeles High School. He was a serious man with little room for humor, opposite of Mr. Edwards, who was upbeat and had been my teacher for three years. Feinstein rarely gave second chances in his classroom. In order for him to even consider the idea, I would have to humble myself and approach him with my heart in hand. I explained to Mr. Feinstein that I had not been able to dedicate the necessary time to write my essay because I had spent most of my time traveling to visit my mother, who was currently living in a shelter forty-five minutes away. It was the first time he and I had ever had a conversation beyond the regular content of our classroom.

While a somewhat humiliating experience, the opportunity to share my story with Mr. Feinstein was a humbling one. It was another character-building lesson for me to recognize my humanity and to ask for help. There were so many times I had felt disappointed and ashamed in my family's request for help. From food stamps to borrowing money, part of my drive came from never wanting to be in that situation myself. I learned a new type of inner strength in asking for a second chance. But I had to be honest with myself about the pain I felt in being separated from my family.

Thankfully, Mr. Feinstein gave me another chance. He told me he appreciated my courage in coming to him with the truth. I spent an entire week rewriting and reviewing a paper on Macbeth, a subject I could have cared less about. I was grateful for the chance to redeem myself and took the exercise seriously. Mr. Feinstein saw my efforts and gave me the passing grade that would allow me to walk across the stage on graduation day. It was the most satisfying news I had received in a while. I would graduate high school.

When I found out that I would be taking part in the culminating ceremony, I felt relieved. As if all the weight I had been carrying had been removed. I left Mr. Feinstein's classroom, running down the hallway and throwing my fist up in the air in celebration. I got to the quad and sat for a minute to catch my breath. With so many students preparing for graduation, there was barely anyone around, which gave me a quiet moment to reflect.

Senior year of high school was one of the toughest years of my life to date. I started the year couch surfing, and, with so much instability in my home life, I allowed those challenges to interfere with my ability to focus. At the same time, I reflected on all those times I woke up early to leave Marvin's house by 5:30am, only to return well past 8pm at night. Despite my mistakes, I had made it, and the hard work was worth it. I was now seeing it all pay off.

In my reflection, I also thought about the people that helped me get to this point. Marvin and his family for giving me a place to stay with no questions asked. For teachers like Mr. Feinstein for giving me a second chance. Mr. Edwards and Mrs. Gibbs for showing me my own potential. And, for other school personnel, like Mrs. Atkins, my high school college counselor.

Earlier that year, I had been fortunate enough to work with Mrs. Atkins, who pushed many students like myself to apply for college. Even when we weren't sure we would be attending, she advised us to be ready just in case.

Mrs. Atkins put together sessions on how to fill out financial aid applications. No one in my family, including my mother, had a clue about filing a FAFSA application. In fact, even reading the application in English was a challenge. My mother tried to support me through the process by attending some of Mrs. Atkins's sessions, but I would end up filling out most of the paperwork myself. I ended up signing my mother's name a few times when I wasn't able to see her in time to complete a form before the deadline.

Mrs. Atkins was committed to getting the highest number of seniors into a four-year university. If students weren't ready, Mrs. Atkins would insist that they start at the junior college level. She inspired us to do better in the classroom so that our grades could never hold us back, while she helped us prepare to fund the next steps of our education by ensuring that money was never the deciding obstacle.

By the time the graduation ceremony came around, I had financial aid and grants ready to go. All thanks to Mrs. Atkins, who had been a significant force in pushing me to continue pursuing higher education.

First High School Diploma in the Family

My graduation ceremony was held on our football field at L.A. High School. In the gym, where we all gathered to get ready to go out onto the field, everyone was grinning from ear to ear. You couldn't walk more than a few steps before a classmate greeted

you with a 'we did it!' high five or a congratulatory hug. I was overwhelmed. I felt an enormous sense of joy and pride.

I took a moment to breathe and thank God as I soaked it all in. I remembered all of the near-death experiences, moments of violence, and tremendous sorrow I had felt over the last four years. I had survived it all.

When it was time, the Los Angeles High School senior class lined up and filed out into the audience to take our assigned seats in the center of our friends and family. The ceremony commenced, and I waited patiently for my name to be called to walk across the stage. After each name was called, cheers, shouts and horns could be heard from the surrounding guests in the bleachers. I prepared myself for silence, unsure if anyone from my family had made it. I thought to myself that perhaps some of my soccer teammates would be cheering for me as I walked across the stage.

To my surprise, however, when I heard "Moisés Linares" announced, noise erupted from a corner of the bleachers well beyond anything my mother could make alone. I looked up to

124

see my whole family cheering my name. My grandmother, sisters, cousins, and aunts had all come and were chanting my name with jubilation. I had no idea how they all found transportation to this corner of the city, but there they were to cheer me on. I looked just long enough to see my mother's mouth say that she loved me until my principal moved me along. I left the stage waving to them. I got emotional knowing they had sacrificed to be there to celebrate my accomplishment that day.

My family celebrates my High School graduation at Los Angeles High School.

We all gathered in my Tia Yesenia's living room to celebrate together with pizza and Pepsi. It was ironic that we were celebrating my graduation in the same neighborhood I had been asked to leave a year before in order to protect my life. I might not have ever seen the day if my aunt had not risked her safety and begrudgingly asked me to leave.

Tio Oscar pulled me aside to talk to me like a father spoke to a son. He told me he was proud of me and that his trip to the States with my mother had not been in vain. While this moment was a huge achievement for our family, he urged me to keep going. He explained how much he admired my discipline and warned me never to lose my drive for more.

Despite Tio Oscar's own choices and those of his sons, I always looked up to him like a father. I could never remember a time when he had let me down, despite him being a man of little words. I let him reminisce on my family's trek to Los Angeles as a means to relate with the courage of completing something special. It was a profound moment between us.

My mother let my uncle finish his nostalgic story with pride, taking the seat beside me in the corner of Tia Yessie's living room. She took both of my hands in her own and said a small prayer of gratitude. With tears in her eyes, she congratulated me on being the first in our family to graduate high school. My mother described the great joy she felt by me accomplishing things that she had always envisioned for me. She ended the conversation by saying that she couldn't wait to attend my college graduation in just a few more years.

I allowed those words to sink deeply into my heart. My family and I were planning for college together.

First-Generation College Student

A few weeks after my graduation, more good news fell upon our family when my mother secured a house through the Section 8 program. The place was only five blocks away from the home we had been evicted from, a sobering yet hopeful reminder to our family about how far we had come.

It was the first time in two years we had a place big enough for all eight of us to live together. Section 8 housing had requirements similar to the welfare program, so besides preparing for college, I was also supporting my mom with visits to the government fund office to help with paperwork and translations.

I visited the Section 8 office several times with my mother at the beginning of our stay to get things situated. Each time we went to the office, I became more and more acquainted with the staff working there and built up a rapport. By our fifth visit, the office manager pulled me aside before we left and asked if I was interested in a job. The position would pay between $16 and $18 per hour, almost double the hourly rate of any minimum wage job I might get at my age with my level of experience. The manager explained that this was only an entry-level salary and that with time and experience, I could easily progress to higher-paying positions within the county.

I thanked the manager and told her I would need a few days to think about her generous offer. On the bus ride home, I began thinking about the experience I might gain in the position and, more importantly, how I could help my mother with rent and bills to keep our home.

My mother interrupted my thoughts as we were approaching our stop. She asked me what the Section 8 office manager had pulled me aside to talk about. In the one-hour commute back to our new home, I had decided that I would take the job and that college would still be there for me once I had gotten my family back on stable footing. I dodged the question for a moment, using our departure from the bus to buy me some time. I didn't want to disappoint my mother after all the excitement surrounding my graduation.

On our walk home, I mentioned that the office manager had offered me a job with a great wage, one that would help our family stay together. Before I could even mention the manager's promise of upward mobility, my mother immediately shut down the idea.

"No. You're going to college," she said. And just like that, the discussion was over.

My mother didn't fully understand the concept of college. From our work with the FAFSA officer, she got familiar with some of the minor details involved. However, for the most part, college was a mystery to a family that was forced to prioritize work over an education. At the very least, she recognized that college was the gateway to a better life in the future. Working in the place of college was not an option for me at this point.

During my senior year, I was accepted to a university in the same region, California State University Northridge (CSUN), plus a few other schools north of California. Leaving home for college, especially leaving the state, was never really an idea I had even contemplated. Being close to my mother and sisters was something very important to me, and the thought of leaving them was unfathomable.

CSUN was an obvious first choice for me, not only for its proximity but because their journalism program had a great reputation. I had visited the campus back in the fall of 2002, and the students and professors I had met had left a positive impression.

Once my minor distraction from working for the county disappeared, I was left with the challenge of finding daily transportation to campus. I didn't own a car and a daily bus ride to Northridge in the San Fernando Valley would take me almost three hours each way. I was beginning to get discouraged and started to doubt my ability to attend. It didn't seem realistic. I didn't tell my mother this time, but I began to spend my energy on plotting to delay my attendance.

A few days after I decided to delay my college career, I received a phone call from my friend Chris, whom I had known since the 6th grade. Chris and I had grown up playing on the same club team in high school. When Chris attended Hamilton High School, we would play against each other from time to time. Although we had gone to different high schools, we were inseparable during most weekends as teenagers. We would play soccer, attend all the *quinceañeras* — 15th birthday parties for young women — and frequent the local mall together. We were just being teenagers. Chris was one of my closest friends.

That night, Chris asked me if I would consider attending Rio Hondo Community College in Whittier to play soccer. I had never heard of the school. While it was closer than California State University Northridge, it was still a 45-minute drive away from my home.

Chris must have sensed my hesitation and began to insist. He reminded me of how much fun we had playing together as teenagers. He shared that college was a new adventure for him as well. And just like me, his family knew very little about furthering their education. If we went to Whittier together, we could support each other. I took a second longer to contemplate the offer and finally agreed. Soccer would, once again, be a driving force behind most of my decisions to move forward toward new goals.

Upon my acceptance, Chris immediately started to map out our next year. To my great fortune, Chris told me that we could carpool to campus together. I wouldn't need to worry about owning a car for a while. Chris was determined to build a strong soccer team and was calling friend by friend to recruit them to attend Rio Hondo alongside us. It didn't take long for our carpool to grow.

Chris' next recruit was our friend Romulo. Romulo was a year older than us and had been working full-time at a car dealership after his high school graduation. In high school, Romulo was one of the most talked-about players in South Central Los Angeles. He had even been invited to play for the Salvadoran national team. The entire city had been buzzing about the tall, skinny, light-skinned kid who knew how to play. However, Romulo was making good money at his job, and it took Chris a few attempts to convince him to join us in community college. Romulo was also from a family of modest means, so a paycheck meant a lot, but his love of the game eventually over-ruled such practicality.

After a few conversations with Chris, Romulo agreed, and our group expanded to three. Romulo would drive about three miles out of his way each morning to pick me up. It was another reminder for me of how fortunate I was to have great friends. I was also aware of how soccer was a light on a new pathway, not only for me but for my friends as well. The simple sport had brought all three of us young men to a place that our families could not have even dreamed of — it was taking us to college.

The Road to Success Starts Here

We took the summer to prepare for college. We drove to campus together to take academic placement tests and met with the soccer coaches to receive feedback on skills we needed to work on.

In late August, Chris, Romulo, and I arrived at Rio Hondo Community College for our first day of school. It felt similar to the first day of high school. The campus was still an unfamiliar place, and we didn't know what to expect as we wandered in search of our first class.

All three of us were the first in our families to attend school past the 12th grade. Our focus in attending Rio Hondo was primarily to play soccer. However, our awareness that we were breaking barriers for our families was not something any of us could forget. We never spoke about it. It was just something that the three of us carried around like an invisible backpack. It was an extra load that we all felt the weight of yet carried with great responsibility and pride.

Chris, Romulo, and I were together most of the day unless we ran to separate classes. In between classes and practice, we would study together, and we actually enjoyed our schoolwork. We created a rhythm between us that kept us progressing forward.

Our daily lives on campus were different from high school. It was as if the atmosphere had changed to further encourage our achievement. While there was still a designated area where the most fashionable kids gathered to hang out, much like "the spot" at L.A. High, most of the students on campus were looking to excel in their studies. There was no discussion or peer pressure about cutting classes at Rio Hondo. We were all there to work.

We each had a full schedule and were taking six classes per semester. Our competitive nature seeped over from sports into our academics, and we all became obsessed with getting the best grades among our group. During our first semester of college, we lived on campus for almost twelve hours each day. We trained and we studied from Monday to Friday in Whittier.

On the weekends, we spent our time on the field playing games in local leagues, looking to up our fitness for the Rio Hondo team. Soccer continued to fuel our drive for success. We all wanted to continue improving our game. We realized together that soccer could provide bigger opportunities for us to move beyond Rio Hondo. We all wanted something bigger.

A few of our teammates had mentioned the concept of receiving a scholarship from other schools to play soccer with them. If we did well, we might get noticed and asked to play at a bigger school. Such financial aid would also give us the peace of mind to continue with school without burdening our families who couldn't afford to pay for expensive textbooks and tuition.

As a kid, my mother always said, *"Dime con quién andas y te diré quien eres"* — tell me who you hang around with and I will tell you who you are.

At Rio Hondo, you could look at each of us young men and know exactly who we were. Chris and Romulo were rock solid as friends. We all wanted the same thing and worked under similar conditions in our home and family life. We understood each other — our strengths, our challenges that made us better, our commitment to finishing what we started.

This aligned drive provided the support we all needed at different times. We would tutor each other when we needed the extra help. We strategized together about soccer to improve our own games. This usually happened at Chris' home, and his family became like a second family to me and Romulo. We made decisions as a team, always thinking about what the best outcome was for us all.

Eventually, others joined our threesome. Ricky was first, easily catching on to our rhythm of support and challenging one another to step up. Then came Mario, Marvin, and Jimmy.

When we weren't playing soccer or studying, each of us worked a few hours each week just to have a little extra spending money. Chris worked in his mother's office, Romulo returned to the Honda dealership, Ricky helped a local soccer coach, and I started out working at a gas station overnight on the weekends. On Mondays, I would show up to school with very little sleep, having gotten off work just a few hours before class started, and realized that the job was unsustainable.

I juggled a few jobs during the beginning of college but would end up working at Macy's as a part-time employee. Management would place me in the fashion jewelry department, where I sold accessories like watches and purses.

I really disliked working in retail, with the intense pressure to hit our daily sales goals and the entitlement of some customers. But the work taught me a few things about customer service and communication. Working at Macy's and dealing with difficult customers gave me an opportunity to practice my communication skills with strangers. This would be an invaluable skill later in my career.

My second year at Rio Hondo, I got a real taste of the foundations of journalism. A close cousin to my childhood dream of sportscasting, journalism was a vast field that included multiple different specialties. I took a few introductory courses that taught us about the history of journalism and further detailed those different categories that reporters practice. From TV news to radio or print journalism, they were all related to the larger goal of sharing news in compelling ways, but each had its own distinction to captivate target audiences and unique ways of being executed.

My journalism professor was a former sports reporter who had covered a lot of the professional teams in Southern California during his career. His classes were filled with stories from his days reporting on the Los Angeles Angels of Anaheim, the L.A. Dodgers, and Lakers.

I felt an instant connection with Professor Durking, and I found my confidence within the first couple of weeks by listening to his stories. I saw how our lessons would translate into the work. He shared his insight on approaching some of the world's best athletes for interviews. Professor Durking recalled the times he covered the Showtime Lakers in the 1980s. He had interviewed legends like Magic Johnson at the iconic Forum when the team was at its peak. Professor Durking had also covered the Dodgers' last World Series title in 1988. The Dodgers wouldn't win another series after that game until thirty-two years later.

Once again, I started visualizing what life would be like if that dream of being a sports journalist became a reality. I would often stay after class just to listen to Professor Durking share more about his experiences. I was enamored, almost hypnotized.

Professor Durking's class was an inside look into the sports world from someone who had covered the subject for over two decades. His passion, stories, and insights on how to get there were the building blocks that invited me to continue learning. His class provided a roadmap for me to follow. It gave me some action behind the hope that my 7th-grade self, listening to old soccer games on the train tracks walking home from school, could use to propel me forward with a degree in sports journalism.

Within the blink of an eye, two years of college at Rio Hondo had come and gone. Most of us were leaving junior college as honor students, which was an accomplishment for boys that were the first to pursue education beyond high school. After four semesters together, our supportive group of young men from immigrant families was disbanding to move in our respective directions.

Chris was recruited to play soccer for the University of San Francisco up north. Ricky would head to Dominguez Hills to play soccer, while Mario and Jimmy stayed back to finish their courses at Rio Hondo.

At Rio Hondo, in Professor Durking's class, journalism became my new obsession. I was given a chance to play at a four-year university. However, the University of La Verne did not have a journalism program, leading me to decline the offer. Instead,

Romulo and I would enroll in California State University Northridge in the San Fernando Valley.

The carpools, late-night study sessions, work on the field, and time in Chris' kitchen were behind us. It was a bittersweet feeling to move on from the comfort and encouraging camaraderie we gave one another. The friendships we had garnered over those two years, however, made us family. This stability of unwavering love and respect for one another gave us permission to carry our dreams forward.

For the next four months, I commuted from South Central to Northridge in the Valley. The house I lived in while attending Rio Hondo was up for sale, which meant we were once again on the move. While my mother looked for a place for us to live, Chris's mother allowed me to stay on her couch. My education needed to continue regardless of where I lived or the challenges around my living situation.

Without many options, my mother, who was still head of the house, would make a tough choice that would benefit me the most. She would relocate the entire family to the San Fernando Valley. This reduced my commute to Northridge to just a few minutes. It made attending school a lot easier. It also kept my younger sisters away from the dangers of South Central L.A. We were together again.

Northridge was a community with a great reputation for the most part. Rent in the nicer part of the town was out of our Section 8 budget, and the only place we could afford was a small, gated neighborhood called Park Parthenia, more commonly known as *Tijuanita* — Little Tijuana. Tijuanita was made up primarily of Latino residents and, unfortunately for us and those that lived there, the area had an extensive history of crime and murder.

Despite our family's hope of leaving the adversity of South Central's streets, we seemed to have merely swapped one terrifying neighborhood for another. Under our financial restrictions, we had no other options, and I had to come to peace with that reality. It made my start to college at California State University Northridge that much more promising. It was time to get us out of the hood.

California State University Northridge

The California State University Northridge campus was beautiful. The CSUN environment seemed to align with the fresh energy I was filled with. My family was reunited. We were in a stable home, and I was getting so much closer to finishing school and accomplishing the next step of my goals.

Simultaneously, I was nervous about attending CSUN. I no longer had the accountability checks that all of my friends provided at Rio Hondo. Romulo was also attending CSUN, but we had opposite schedules and rarely saw each other. Things were much different from the times we spent every free moment studying together.

The biggest shift, this time, was the cultural shock of attending school with so many white classmates. Prior to CSUN, I had never been in a class with more than one or two white students. The only other time I had ever been around so many white people in one place was usually on the soccer field. Even then, we were on opposite teams. Other than that, I had mostly seen white people in positions of authority, somewhat removed from myself and my family. People like my mother's employers, typically owners of the homes she would clean. Northridge provided me with a novel experience to interact with an entire race of people I had never known. It gave me the chance to learn how the dominant culture in the United States operated every day.

As a kid, I always remember my family acting inferior around white people. My Tia Miriam worked as a nanny for a wealthy white family in both Santa Monica and Beverly Hills. I visited her a few times while she was working and remember never feeling like I belonged. My aunt validated that feeling by telling me to just stay put and not say anything. This was similar to how my mother would ask me to behave around white people as well. It always felt like they were trying to make themselves smaller, and maybe even invisible, so they didn't interfere with their lives. It pained me to see.

When I was old enough to work, I experienced my own feelings of making myself less seen. I would help Chris at his mother's office to move boxes or other heavy office furniture sometimes. I would listen to how his mother's boss would talk about us like we weren't even in the room. Her comments were often geared at making us feel lower, like she was doing us a favor by hiring us.

My interactions at CSUN were different. The differences in culture and heritage between me and my classmates didn't matter to them. If anyone felt any type of way, they didn't show it. It shocked me to be treated as just another student, but I never felt out of place. I knew I had earned my way there and others seemed to see that too.

A group project for an anthropology class would become the first time I actually got to study with white students. I was assigned to a group of four with a white classmate named Henry, who would talk to me as if he had known me for a long time. Surprised, I thought perhaps I had it wrong all along. At least at college, people were more open and didn't stick to preconceived biases. By the end of class, Henry was offering to exchange numbers in order to communicate better outside of class.

My second semester at CSUN, I was required to get a full-time job in addition to the full schedule of classes I was taking. My mother couldn't afford the $1200 portion of the rent we were responsible for after the Section 8 voucher kicked in, and I needed to help her keep our home.

I found a job as a community facilitator with Jay Nolan Community Services, a local nonprofit that assisted children and adults with autism and down syndrome. I worked as often as I could and was able to contribute an extra three hundred dollars each month to our home.

Jay Nolan Community Services became more than a job for me, teaching me great empathy through my work supporting individuals that needed additional assistance integrating into society. It was at Jay Nolan that I met Dennis, a 250 pound 17-year-old with a serious look and a heart of gold. I became Dennis' primary caregiver as part of my work with the community service center.

My job was to make Dennis feel like he was part of the community. We drove around Los Angeles to run errands and explore new things. Dennis had down syndrome. This sometimes prevented others from welcoming him and even caused them to treat him unfairly. People would make mean comments about the way he looked. It always upset me. Dennis was an amazing, fun-loving kid, but it was a reality for Dennis. This reinforced how important my work was for me. I really felt like I could make a difference in Dennis' life.

I played the role of a big brother to Dennis or "Big D" as he came to be known by all my personal friends. Dennis became a little brother and another member of my family. His charisma and dance moves were enough to charm anyone anywhere. You couldn't walk anywhere near a place that was playing music because he would begin to dance. He loved music. Our friendship grew and Dennis would spend a lot of time with my friends and family.

Being around Dennis reminded me of my own blessings. I spoke to him about my own fears, and he always told me it would be okay. Developing a true friendship with Dennis strengthened my compassion for others and myself. Spending time with him helped replace the motivation I got from being so close with the boys at Rio Hondo.

After Dennis, I worked with a few other adults who needed assistance, but none of those experiences matched the connection I had to Big D. I have remained friends with Dennis and his family to this day and am lucky to know him.

Journalism Meets Central American Studies

My mother always told me that everything in life happened for a reason. Each event was a part of God's bigger plan for His Kingdom. If I could accept that and surrender to God's will, I would understand everything. Even when there wasn't an immediate answer, there was a purpose that sooner or later would reveal itself.

I had decided to attend CSUN for journalism and nothing else. I had even turned down an opportunity to play soccer in order to focus on my career goals in sports journalism. One day early in my second semester, I ran into an old soccer rival from high school walking through the campus halls. We said hello and spoke about the classes we were taking now at CSUN. In our casual conversation, Jairo mentioned he was headed to his next class soon on the Diaspora of Central America. Jairo was also a Salvadoran American who grew up in a rough neighborhood in Los Angeles. Like me, soccer had been the driving reason he chose sports and education over selling drugs, fighting, and everything else.

I was finished for the day and decided to observe Professor Douglas Carranza's class that day. There were very few seats available, leaving me to sit right in front of the professor.

Professor Douglas Carranza was a Salvadoran man with long black hair and a great sense of humor. Professor Carranza spoke in such an eloquent and animated way that it felt like everything he said was a piece of spoken word poetry. His stories that day drew everyone in, and it immediately made sense why there were barely any seats available in his class. He made learning history fun. His jokes had the entire class roaring with laughter.

I was captivated and wanted more. When Professor Carranza's class ended that day, I went to the registrar's office immediately to add his class to my schedule. My interest in the history of my family's country had always been there, but I never connected the idea that I could learn about my culture and history in college. Just like my mother had always reminded me, it appeared I was meant to run into Jairo to bring me to Professor Carranza's class.

At the time, all I knew about El Salvador was what my mother and grandmother had told me over the years. It was fascinating to me that an entire class would be dedicated to the study of a region that birthed my mother, grandmother, uncles, and aunts. Cal State Northridge was the first university in the United States that offered a minor that focused on Central America. Other programs around the country had a few classes that centered on Latin American history, but CSUN was leading the way for a fast-emerging group of people that was often ignored. The Central American Studies department was also growing fast, and it was on the verge of offering a four-year degree.

At the time I decided to minor in Central American studies, close to one million Salvadorans had made their way to the United States. By 2019, that number would get closer to a million and a half. The wars in Central America during the 1980s resulted in political and economic instability in the region that caused droves of people to migrate north. A decade later, migration would be prompted by natural disasters, like Hurricane Mitch in 1998, which ruined part of Honduras and Nicaragua, or a series of earthquakes that devastated El Salvador in 2001.

After the first semester with Professor Carranza, I declared a minor in Central American studies. It felt like the perfect way to honor my family members after all they had endured to bring me to this point. I also wanted to know more about where my family came from. I knew about the food and had heard a lot about the violence they had escaped, but I was curious about the history, the art, and the economy of El Salvador.

In the program, I was taught by professors of Central American descent. Prior to this, I had never met Central American educators in Los Angeles. When I thought about Central Americans, I always envisioned my family. Hard workers doing manual labor work like construction, cleaning houses, selling food informally, or janitorial work around the city. Seeing professionals that came from places like El Salvador and Guatemala was powerful. It was reinforcement that as a first-generation American, I was capable of doing so much with my life.

Majoring in journalism and selecting to minor in Central American studies gave me a full course load. I loved both subjects and thought about ways I might merge both areas of interest. I knew sports would always provide some options. My escape from gangs in middle school watching old soccer games of the El Salvador national team reminded me of that option. I felt a pull to do something more. I wanted others to see my people for the hardworking, kind, loving, and creative people we were.

Journalism was a means of telling stories to the greater public. By combining the areas of study, I was offered a mechanism to tell stories about the often invisible communities, like the Central American community, living in Los Angeles and other parts of the country. These stories were rarely ever told, and when a Central American was featured on the news, it typically involved a report about gang activity or some other crime of circumstance. At best, Central Americans were portrayed as victims, but they were never the heroes. Even with that being true, for every "positive" story of a Central American, you had ten negative ones.

I wanted to tell another story, like one of my friends from Rio Hondo being the first in their families to graduate from high school and go on to college. To tell stories about how strong and brave our families were to escape violence and travel to the United States in search of a better life. To talk about the kids I knew from my neighborhood using soccer to cope with difficult situations at home and still making it to school. We were a people with resilience, and that was a story worth telling.

Without soccer, I got more involved on campus with student activity groups and quickly joined the Central American United Student Association (CAUSA). I was taking a full load of courses, working almost forty hours per week, and volunteering time with CAUSA hosting events and programs to support Central American communities locally and abroad.

My major in journalism demanded a lot of my time and was not concerned with my student activities, my job, or my minor in Central American studies. This was real training to make it in a cut-throat industry, and my professors were unforgiving of excuses.

Professor Jim Hill was a former reporter with twenty-five years of experience, including ten years as a correspondent for CNN. His class required a significant amount of reading to stay up to date with the news, much of which was expected to be done outside of class. Professor Hill wanted his students to learn good habits that would allow them to become reporters one day.

We were tested twice a week with quizzes about current events. He also required us to submit a weekly paper summarizing top news events. I was so over-scheduled that I didn't prioritize reading early in the morning and got in the habit of completing my work before class.

Professor Hill noticed my lack of discipline and wasted little time telling me about the areas I needed to work on. Professor Hill was not one to bite his tongue when he gave advice, and it was a tough reality to face that I was falling back into old patterns of losing focus. Despite all of Professor Hill's subtle warnings for me to get back on track, I received my worst college grade at the end of the year — a C.

This was enough for me to snap back into reality. Here I was in college, with a professor with real-world journalism experience, throwing the opportunity away. This would be my one and only stumble at CSUN. I re-enrolled in Professor Hill's course and took things seriously. I stopped attending so many social events and cut back on my hours at work. I also made Professor Hill my mentor.

My second year in his class, I started the year with a meeting in Professor Hill's office. I asked him what I could do to excel in his class. With some hesitation, I asked for feedback on what I did wrong the year prior. In true Professor Hill form, he had direct feedback for me. Professor Hill told me to pay attention to the details. While it was important to pay attention when I showed up to class, Professor Hill reminded me that much of the learning would be done during my studying time. I needed to pay attention to details when I edited reports or coordinated interviews.

When the first meeting was over, I thanked Professor Hill for his time. I think he respected my initiative to come to him for advice and my ability to soak it in. I listened to him. I took notes and I didn't get emotional. I left with an invitation for me to come back anytime to receive feedback.

For the rest of the year, Professor Hill would show me examples of his own work and the methods he used to get there. I set up regular meeting times outside of class to soak in everything he showed me. Outside of my meetings and class time, I went over my work several times to flush out all the fine details. I proofread papers and emails at least three to four times before I considered them good enough to turn in or send out. With Professor Hill's mentorship, I was becoming a professional and a master at my craft.

As a first-generation college student, I was still learning. I was thankful for the teachers along the way who taught me I could focus and, with discipline, get closer to my dream. Mr. Edwards, Mrs. Gibbs, and now Professor Hill were supporting me in ways that my family weren't able to.

Professor Hill would teach several of my journalism classes while at CSUN. Time with Professor Hill would prove to be something like an apprenticeship. With each class, I was getting better and better at the details and learning the nuances to reporting a story in a more interesting way. I was perfecting my journalism skills from a master teacher.

Eventually, I declared a double major in Broadcast Journalism and Central American studies after the Central American Studies department announced it would now offer a Bachelor of Arts. I was one of thirty students to declare the major. The double major meant I had to stay in school for an extra year, which I gladly welcomed as an investment in my future and more time to get ready for my professional career. My last two years at CSUN were the most exciting times of my academic journey. Almost every single one of my classes was a Central American studies or journalism course. I got to use the extra time in school to soak in the two subjects that mattered most to me while getting the opportunity to hone my broadcasting skills.

Manzanita Hall

Opened in 2003, Manzanita Hall, the broadcast journalism building, was my favorite building on campus. It was a contemporary structure, shaped like a spaceship, that had replaced the older building destroyed by the 1994 Northridge earthquake. Room 150 of Manzanita Hall was always bustling with students coming in and out. The room was outfitted as a small TV studio with cameras, microphones, and editing stations arranged in different corners.

The world of journalism was shifting into a digital space. While we still learned all of the traditional methods of recording, tapes were phasing out, and professors were preparing us to be flexible and adaptable for new things, including things that were still unknown at the time. CSUN professors wanted us to be experienced in both worlds of journalism so that we could be successful in anything.

In Manzanita Hall, we were training to do it all — record, edit, write, and produce. We were each becoming our own "one-man band." For many journalists, the odds of having to do everything yourself were very high. Starting out in their careers, they often reported for smaller stations first to gain experience. This meant reporting with little to no budget for any additional personnel.

CSUN's journalism program was at the forefront of preparing us for the industry. While we were marching to our "one-man-band" in room 150, students at neighboring schools were still working in groups of three to mimic roles of producer, cameraman, and reporter. We learned how to do it all on our own because of the looming shifts to the economy and job market demands.

One of the first things we learned was editing. A skillset that would benefit a lot of us starting off in TV after graduation. Next, hands-on classes allowed us to experiment with different camera techniques to pick up the best angles to the most basic of shots. We determined what made a good visual report, understanding wide, medium, and close-ups shots, all to tell the best story.

Room 150 was the place where I would see myself on camera for the first time. Just weeks after learning some basics, we were sent out to record mini reports around campus. For the assignment, we had to interview other students on campus about any subject. We had to stop them and ask for permission and also had to set up our own equipment once they said yes.

Watching myself on camera was thrilling. It felt like my dreams were really coming true. It was also a terrifying experience. Watching myself, I witnessed firsthand just how much work I still needed to do. I was visually nervous on camera. I spoke in a monotone so flat and dull I wanted to doze off watching myself. I was watching the total opposite of an experience I thought I would give my audiences.

In my mind, I had imagined my on-air persona would have a polished presence on camera, with a powerful voice and a humble character. I was going to be the reporter you wanted to watch because I was approachable, like a friend, and dependable to always give you the truth in a manner you understood. The exercise made me realize I needed some serious practice. Soon, I discovered I was not the only one that needed some refinement. No one in my class was born a professional and getting better would only come with constant repetition. That first assignment sobered me to the years of hard work and dedication it would take to become the professional I envisioned.

Professor Lincoln, the journalism department lead for all introductory courses, reiterated the importance of giving ourselves time to learn. He and the rest of the professors pushed everyone to put in the time to get better. Professor Lincoln gave us tips to improve and told us to practice our delivery in front of a mirror every single day. Good journalists never gave up or took NO for an answer.

My final four semesters at CSUN were the perfect opportunity to marry my interests of broadcast journalism and Central American studies. We were given flexibility in the stories we found and covered in journalism courses. The professors only wanted to make sure that we were capturing the details of camera angles, editing, and, most of all, telling a captivating story. We were all given access to camera equipment and told to have fun.

With the bulky camera equipment of that time, I would haul the massive cameras all over Los Angeles to cover stories about people like my family and friends. We covered the Central American Independence Festival in McArthur Park, an event that brought hundreds together to celebrate the countries in Central America they had left behind. We told stories about places like Jay Nolan Community Services, a community-based organization, where staff and volunteers did amazing work to help people with disabilities.

Our final roles in Manzanita Hall were to produce and report for Valley View Newscast, our school's news channel. With support from professors, students ran the newscast — from choosing the stories, framing studio shots, editing, and writing scripts. Valley View News was a proper introduction to what a newsroom looked and felt like.

At Valley View News, I got closer to Jahmai Webster. Jahmai and I had several classes together but had never really had a conversation until our last year. We bonded over our love of sports, being the two in our class most motivated to tell every possible story about local sports before the year was over. I felt the similar competitive spirit I had developed with Chris and Romulo at Rio Hondo. We pushed each other to do better, supported one another, and once again, so much of our group dynamic was centered around sports.

Jahmai and I covered soccer, basketball, boxing, and tennis. I loved all sports, but my passion had always been soccer. Working shoulder to shoulder with Jahmai pushed me to prove that I could expand my area of expertise and versatility. I could cover other major sports, including all of those played at CSUN. We had everything except football. It was good practice to keep our competitive edge. Stations around the country wanted someone who could cover it all, and many times, soccer was pretty far down the list of desired areas of coverage.

Beyond sports and things on campus, we covered other things in the city. Jahmai and I collaborated on the first-ever on-camera investigative report on day workers in the city. For weeks, we went out into the city to speak to people standing in front of home improvement retailer stores and construction sites looking for jobs. It was out of our comfort zone, but it showed we were more than just sports reporters. This would be the biggest and hardest assignment we had ever taken on. It took us weeks to write and put everything together on camera. It took hours of editing on three different computers to finish the segment.

By the end of my time at Manzanita Hall, Jahmai and I would produce fifteen reports each in a single semester. Not all of them were great, but our persistence and dedication were there. It was proof that we could be real reporters.

The First Ever

College graduation day was a huge celebration for my family. My high school culmination had been a tremendous accomplishment, but college was so much bigger. It was the moment many of my aunts and uncles had imagined when they left El Salvador in the 1980s. They were witnessing one of their nephews graduating from college. I was accomplishing something as a first-generation American. They fought hard to get to the United States in order for me to do this.

I was the first in my family to graduate with a four-year college degree. It was validation for all of the sacrifices my mother had made to get me here. The day I picked up my cap and gown, I couldn't help but remember the many times we moved around Los Angeles from my kindergarten to college years.

I would take part in two separate graduation ceremonies, one with the journalism department and the second with the department of Central American studies. It was a prideful moment for me to have public declarations celebrating both my career dreams and my family heritage. In both ceremonies, I wore a custom cap that read *para mi familia* — for my family. My eyes got watery as I walked across each stage. I waved at my family, shouting that we had done it.

Graduating from college was more than receiving a diploma. It was an accomplishment I made after setting the goal and going after it with determination and tenacity. For a period of about five years, I worked hard every day. I kept the memory of my family's journey to the United States with me, always remembering what had been sacrificed to give me this opportunity. Everywhere I went on campus, the history of my mother's 3,000-mile trek went with me. When school got tough, I pushed through, remembering what my family had been through. They were a huge part of the reason I never allowed myself to give up.

Before beginning my journey in search of a four-year degree, I knew I could either get up and fight for my goals or sit around and allow life to punch me senseless. As an avid sports enthusiast, I followed all the greats, including the boxer, Muhammed Ali.

Ali once said, "Champions are made from something they have deep inside them, a desire, a dream, a vision." The quote stuck with me, tucked in the back of my mind alongside my family's pursuit of a better life. It was one of many things sports continue to teach me.

Despite all the opportunities that the United States offered, the country still fell short in providing equal possibilities for all of its people. Messages about Black and Brown communities and their young men repeatedly told the story of violence, scarcity, and death. By these standards, society expected me to fail. It was a message that looped for me throughout school and in every new neighborhood we moved to, but it was one I had rejected years ago. Instead, taking Ali's advice, I saw myself as a champion. There was greatness within me that I could always access. Overcoming so many challenges was my version of picking myself up each time I got knocked down.

Apart from the two diplomas I would receive for finishing school, I knew I was doing something much bigger. I was part of a bigger promise that the boys from Rio Hondo and I had started. I was my brother's keeper, and my finishing school would create a ripple effect that pushed others around me to consider going to college. Of our Rio Hondo squad, Chris obtained a degree from USF, and Romulo and Ricky would do the same from Cal State Dominguez Hills.

Eventually, those ripples would reach others I cared for from my childhood, like my friend José. Known in the streets of South Central as "Shorty," José began pursuing a college degree at twenty-five years old.

José and I had lost touch after our middle school days riding in the back of Coach Minor's truck. We reconnected briefly during high school but didn't stay in touch. I was working with Mrs. Atkins to apply for financial aid and looking to make college a reality. He had gotten wrapped up in some of the local party crew and hadn't made school a priority.

151

In my second year of college, José and I ran into each other playing recreational soccer. Watching peers like me avoid gangs and drugs for something more productive left him tormented. He explained to me that he wanted more than what the street offered him and had been considering going back to school. But, like so many people from our neighborhood, he was afraid to enter the unknown and leave his comfort zone. At this time, his age was a barrier for him. José had to start from ground zero, and he feared he might be too old to complete college.

José's final push came when his younger sister Rosa became the first in his family to attend college. Now José had two people in his life to support him through this life-changing decision. Both Rosa and I were there for him anytime he sought advice. José learned to balance a full-time job with a full course load the same way I had done years before.

José also had to block out the naysayers in the hood. Many in his neighborhood saw college as a waste of time and let José know that every time they saw him. Each time he felt like quitting, he would call me or Rosa, and we would talk him back to his goals.

Like me, José would make the tough choice of separating himself from the hood he had lived in his whole life. It was challenging to move between such different worlds each day and remain strong and focused. In the same way, Chris and Romulo had held me accountable at Rio Hondo, I supported José through his first few years in school.

I checked on him frequently to see how he was doing in his classes. At times I felt like I was listening to myself whenever José would express his concerns and challenges with specific classes or schedule balancing. One afternoon, José called to share a specific assignment he was working on. He needed details about journalism and my career goals to use in a presentation he was giving to class. After providing the information he needed, I congratulated his continued efforts and asked more about the assignment. He told me the assignment focused on someone from his neighborhood whom he considered a success.

After hanging up with José, his words sank in. I was no longer only doing this for my family and immediate circle of friends. Other people from my neighborhood were beginning to pay attention to my journey and using me as an example of how they might embark on their own paths. Through messages like these, God continued to validate to me that my purpose was so much bigger than myself.

José went on to transfer to CSUN, following a similar path to mine. He graduated nine years after he had first enrolled in community college. José was thirty-four years old and proved anything is possible when you want it bad enough. He would become an example for adults in our neighborhood as well, showing them that sometimes all it takes is a little courage to get things done.

Courage was something I was getting used to mustering after years of overcoming financial instability, homelessness, and institutional barriers. I would need it because things were just getting started.

PART 3
A Cut-throat Industry

The dream of many aspiring reporters is to gain instant popularity as soon as they begin. Popularity lifts ratings and increases a reporter's value to any station. This means more choices in where one can work, as well as more money.

I was no different. I dreamed of starting my career working in Los Angeles, my home, but also the second-largest market in the country. My reality, however, was something completely different. After graduation, like so many of my peers, I had to search for opportunities and would wait many years before landing my first full-time TV job.

By the time I became a full-time reporter, almost all of my CSUN classmates working in TV were quitting their jobs. The TV reporter gig was so much harder than any of them had expected. You had to hustle just to get steady work, and even when you did, the pay usually wasn't good enough to stay in the business long term. Journalists working in smaller markets might earn $20,000 to $25,000 annually, just enough to pay rent and buy groceries. Many broadcasting hopefuls leave the industry in search of better-paying jobs in more consistent fields just a few years after they begin.

My first job in the industry was a production assistant role. I got the job through networking during my last year of college. I learned early that half the battle is knowing the right people; relationships are key. A simple hello email or text message went a long way. It was a lesson every professor and professional I had ever met mentioned repeatedly. I took the advice to heart and quickly became the kid who would reach out immediately and consistently after meeting you. I wanted to be someone they would remember so I could be top of mind when any position was open.

My practices led me to a part-time position as an editor and writer at Direct TV Sports. I was required to meet segment editing deadlines and write sports news alerts for the on-screen ticker. After working hard and learning for a few months, the team offered me a full-time position. Although I needed the money, I declined the offer. I appreciated what I learned there but knew the job wasn't the right fit for me. The job had little to do with video production and would've pushed me further away from my goals. I had a different career trajectory in mind.

Not long after I declined the position at Direct TV Sports, I landed my first full-time job at Zorro Sports, a bilingual sports network. As a young professional, Zorro Sports was an ideal next step. It was a national network with a significant reach in all the major markets in the country. I knew I would learn a lot and make some real connections in the position.

During my first interview, I made it clear that my primary goal was to be in front of a camera as a reporter. I discovered soon after that being so boldly honest was not the best approach for a first interview. While the vice president of the channel was intrigued by my drive and determination, my soon-to-be supervisors laughed in my face. I was interviewing for a production job. While moving to reporter was possible, admitting I saw the production position as a mere steppingstone came off as presumptuous.

At the end of the interview, the company was clear that on-camera opportunities were possible and that the production job could serve as an entry point for me. They also gave me feedback to stay humble because this was a cut-throat industry, and the reality of making it in front of the camera was rare for most. I took away the advice about humility and that there was a chance. I left the rest. My 24-year-old self was so full of energy and hope nothing else seemed to matter.

Once I started, however, I got my first cold dose of industry reality. Because journalism and broadcasting are difficult fields to make it in, competition and jealousy ran rampant. Superiors would make sure that I was as far away from an on-camera opportunity as possible. They knew what I wanted, so they challenged me by creating barriers. It was a rocky beginning at Zorro.

One thing my supervisors didn't know about me, however, was just how hard I had already worked to get in front of them. They knew nothing about my drive to stay on my high school campus from 5am to 7pm just to get my work done. They didn't know I battled for my life some days just to make it past the violence at school. They didn't know just how much courage I had worked up to bring me into that office.

I wasn't sure how I would do it, but I knew that I could make it happen simply by my sheer willingness to put in the work. I started by perfecting the job I was hired to do. I kept my head low and did my work with excellence. I wanted to keep things running smoothly for my team without attracting too much attention. I logged game after game, edited highlights, and prepared upcoming shows. I ran the play-by-play announcers their papers-shot sheets with all the information they would talk about during halftime. I made them look great by always being on time.

At Zorro, I met Julio, an assistant producer of Honduran descent I was assigned to shadow to learn the ropes. Julio was a master at editing shows and highlights. He had access to all of the studio's best pieces of equipment. There were very few Central Americans there and Julio was excited to have me. He wanted to see me succeed. Julio and I hit it off immediately.

A few weeks after I started working with Julio, I asked him if he could help get me access to practice reporting in front of a camera or microphone. Julio asked me more about my goals, both to cover himself and to learn more about my aspirations to become a reporter. He was thrilled to hear about my childhood dream. Julio would often tell me, "you can do it, *chiquitito*" — little guy — but always reiterated that my dream required a lot of hard work and sacrifice.

Whenever I had a chance, I would complete my responsibilities with Julio and look for small windows to hone my skills. This often meant coming in earlier and staying late after work. I also found other ways to insert my skills by always volunteering for voice-over test recordings the studio needed to get the sound right.

As I practiced, Julio told me about a well-known Cuban American sports anchor that had worked his way up from the production team to reporting on camera. Martino Trojaski was a former production assistant turned superstar, reporting on everything from Major League Soccer to hosting daily soccer shows that aired throughout the nation.

After six months at Zorro, I got the opportunity to work with Martino for a short period of time. Martino was an agreeable man who answered the numerous questions I sprinkled throughout our work.

Martino's stories offered guidance to me in a similar manner as the informal mentorships I had experienced in school. It showed me a possible path from production to a position on air. Most importantly, it showed me that someone just like me made it in front of the camera. Martino's journey encouraged me to believe that I could follow him and do the same.

Martino was like a living Roger Bannister. In the 1950s, Bannister became a world hero for doing something considered impossible. On May 6, 1954, Bannister broke the record for the fastest mile in under four minutes. He paced at 3:59:04, setting a new world record. Prior to Bannister, this feat was deemed impossible. Many other runners flirted with the record in an attempt to break it but would fall seconds short of the goal. In Oxford, England, Bannister proved the impossible was possible.

Running the mile in under four minutes would be repeated thousands of times after Bannister. He had laid the foundation for future runners. Now, a mile completed in under four minutes is the norm.

Martino felt like a real-life Bannister. Moving from production to reporting on TV was not seen as a realistic path for anyone working in the industry. However, Martino had a dream, and what others deemed a realistic path did not apply to him. He set his mind on the goal and accomplished the unthinkable.

Martino had the type of character many people were drawn to. His desire to become a big personality in the sports world seemed like a logical way for him to use his gifts. Martino moved from production assistant to a position as an anchor in a matter of months at Zorro. Not long after he finished his first on-air segment, Martino would quickly rise to be one of the top soccer voices in the U.S.

Observing Martino while I assisted him, I instantly took notice of his focus, his eye for detail, and his overall drive. He invested hours of his free time to become a better announcer, reporter, and anchor. This dedication to practice, I learned, was something he started back as a production assistant. He had started the job of announcing long before anyone knew his name.

There was a sharp contrast in how I felt after spending time with Martino versus my other colleagues. Many of my peers at Zorro came to work only so they could pay their bills. Very few of the people around me had a genuine passion for the work. Some didn't seem to be excited about much at all.

I felt drained after being around co-workers with no goals. On the other hand, each time I left Martino, I felt inspired and energized to try something new with my reporting style. I needed to break away from the negative environment and set myself apart from every Zorro employee without direction, especially those who continued to laugh at my dream of being on camera.

Instead of being social, I would wander around the studio, finding motivation by listening to reporters in each recording booth. I observed professionals in every free minute I had to study different styles and to give myself a visual reminder of my professional goals. The station served as my laboratory to learn and practice to prepare for my next move.

With practice came confidence, and soon Julio allowed me to record unofficial promos for Major League Soccer games whenever he was leading production. My work never aired, but the experience gave me a chance to feel what reporting for games would be like in real-time. Julio and I would match video with my voice-over to simulate the completion of a real piece. Julio would also offer me valuable feedback about my performance. Zorro Sports served as an apprenticeship for my reporting dream.

After six months, my responsibilities at the station increased. I started producing shows that only required a voice-over artist and translations from English to Spanish and vice versa. The talent was not required to be in front of the camera for these shows. I was assigned to work on the SAP production of many of the most popular shows that aired on the channel.

For the next year and a half, I produced my own game broadcasts at the station the same way Martino had done in his rise from production to on-air superstar. Every night after 10pm, when Zorro colleagues had left the station, I checked into the recording booth to practice a few more hours. I would use my mornings to prepare the line-ups and notes I practiced in the evening.

From these late-night sessions, I selected my best work to put on tape for a demo. This demo served as a piece I would use for feedback from other professionals at Zorro. I even brought the tape home to play for my uncles, who were the most honest critics I knew.

Despite all the hours I put into my demo tape, I was still learning and, many times, the feedback I received was harsh to hear. Some reporters at Zorro even told me that I simply didn't have it in me. Such comments would have been demoralizing for most, but I worked to keep my ego out of it and focused on the bits of criticism I could use to get better. Determination to achieve my dream gave me the strength to return to the booth every chance I got. I used the persistence of my Abuela Rosa Emília to fuel me. If there was something I understood, it was that no one else was going to make this dream a reality but me.

False Idols

During my time at Zorro Sports, I met a lot of great talent, including some announcers who had been around for decades and others who were up and coming. At one point, Brandon B, a play-by-play announcer I had been following for years, was hired to call games for the station. He was one of my favorite broadcasters from Argentina who was on the rise in the United States.

Brandon had the "it" factor that screamed superstar-in-the-making. His style was unique, and he had a way with reading the tempo of a game. He made the most boring games sound exciting. He made you want to watch. I admired Brandon's talent and kept an eye on his career.

When I learned about Brandon's new gig at the station, I prepared questions to keep on hand in case I ever got the opportunity to ask him something. Fortunately, I was assigned to a project he was working on and would get to see him every weekend. For our first encounter, I must have appeared like a kid meeting one of his favorite athletes for the first time. I was excited and nervous and fumbled around to remember my questions. But before I even had a chance to ask anything, Brandon waved me off and made me feel invisible. It was not the reaction I imagined coming from a guy I modeled myself after as a young journalist. Even some of the most famous broadcasters would entertain a question or two. I was disappointed.

For almost three months, Brandon never said hello and would only address the main producers and other leaders on the project. No matter how hard I tried to casually strike up a conversation with him, he never replied. I was crushed.

Before my job at Zorro, I thought everyone who worked on camera was just as nice as they seemed on TV. I learned about another side of the TV business I knew very little about from Brandon B. The occasional big ego. He would become the reflection of a person I would never want to become in my career. My family had taught me better manners, and I had learned great humility from watching them as a child. I remembered how invisible I felt in the homes of the people my mother and aunts cleaned for and thought back to the treatment they received. I knew firsthand that some of the kindest, hardworking, and loving people did not have the highest titles. To forget my humility would be to lose who I was fundamentally as a person.

Brandon would eventually stop working for the company as his holier-than-thou attitude created conflict with superiors who had power at Zorro. He would fall from a promising career in sports journalism to vacant opportunities and a bad reputation with a large network. Brandon B was a reminder of how ego can destroy all that is important. I thought back to my supervisor's reactions during my job interview. Seeing how my straightforwardness could have easily been misconstrued as entitlement, I better understood their reasons. Being on camera was something you had to work hard for, but even if you managed it, it didn't make you better than anyone else. I would never cross paths with Brandon B again, but the experience changed how I would build my career within this industry.

In direct response to my frustration with Brandon's indifference towards me, I doubled down on serving others. I helped interns excited about starting a career in sports TV. I invested time in getting to know them and asking about their ambitions. I supported them when things they needed were within my reach.

I got to know an intern named Franco very well, and he later became a friend. I knew my way around the studio, and much like Julio was to me, I served as Franco's guide to learning on real equipment during network downtimes. Franco eventually served as my color analyst for the late-night demos I was developing during his internship.

The sharp contrasts in experiences with Brandon B and Franco happened in what would be the final few months of my time at Zorro. My technical learning at Zorro was getting stagnant, and I had started to look for other opportunities. However, God knew I had more to learn from my time there and led me down paths that would test my character. These were lessons that would challenge my integrity and force me to decide who I wanted to be, both on camera and off.

Create Your Own Opportunity

In 2008, my younger cousin Gerson had been signed to the Major League Soccer team Chivas U.S.A. in the Under 18 player squad. A year later, he earned a spot on the top team and continued to excel. His professional career was off to a great start and, despite no requested interviews yet, I knew he would start gaining attention soon. Since, like me, Gerson had grown up in the gang-infested neighborhood of South Central, his success made an inspiring feature. So I decided to produce a story with the intention of getting it aired during the halftime show of an upcoming Chivas U.S.A. game.

I pitched the idea to producers and the vice president of the channel. By this time, I had already taken the time to develop the storyline and coordinated the production logistics to make the approval process for managers as easy as possible. A report of this magnitude would be invaluable for my career, especially at this point. I made sure to have everything in order and prayed on a yes.

Zorro producers loved my idea and were interested in the story. However, they were not comfortable with me being the person to tell it on camera. I got the approval to produce the segment, but not to be the journalist featured on video. I stood my ground, explaining how my connection with the player would provide more authentic content. I told them I needed to produce and star in the feature. Otherwise, I would not give Zorro the exclusive. I left the office with an inconclusive decision. It was a very risky move on my end, but my dream was on the hook, and I knew this was my chance to reel it in.

A few days after the pitch meeting, I was called back into the office. Terrified, I went in with my head held high, still ready to fight for my plan. But that preparation was unnecessary. The producers said yes. This was what I had visualized from the moment I walked into the Zorro studios. Spearheading this assignment for a major network would add tremendous value to my credibility and resume. I was elated.

The day of the interview, I arrived at Gerson's house and immediately saw Martino Trojaski getting out of his car. My gut told me to expect a curveball, so I took a lap around the house before reporting for duty. Upon entry to the shoot, I quickly learned that Martino would be leading the English portion of the interview. I would only be allowed to handle the Spanish version.

Being a bilingual journalist gave me an advantage. It would make me an easy hire to use the same talent in both English and Spanish broadcasts. However, Zorro wanted a big name for my idea. With Martino presenting in English, my language skills wouldn't gain the on-camera credentials I needed.

I had to watch on the sidelines as Martino stumbled through the interview. He had shown up unprepared and instead relied on all the notes and questions I had drafted for the segment. He was unfamiliar with the information. My data, facts, and vision were foreign to him. I watched my carefully crafted concept unfold under Martino's clumsy delivery for a sloppy story at best.

To add insult to injury, the station later decided to only air the English version of the story. But I had a different plan. Throughout my time at this place, I heard every single reason possible why my goals wouldn't work out, from not having the traditional deep sports announcer voice to not having the TV look for the job. Supervisors and producers would tell me I was a smart kid, but I wouldn't make it past a producer job. Not willing to accept defeat, I told myself that I would not stay put with my arms crossed, waiting for something to happen. Life had repeatedly taught me that I had to take what was mine without regrets or looking back. A lot of hard work had gone into obtaining the interview and recording the footage for the story. I had done a lot, if not most, of the work myself. I went back to the station, wrote a script, edited the interview, and completed the report with the help of a few colleagues. I watched it about ten times and made sure it was as good as it could possibly be.

Gameday arrived, and I had it all planned out in my head. I was going to be on TV for the first time in my career. Right before the first half ended, I walked to the control room, and I spoke to the producer. I told him the vice president of the channel had instructed me to give him the video report to air live during the halftime show. The vice president of the channel had left an hour earlier and was no longer in the building to confirm what I was saying. There was also little to no time to check the report before it aired. The producer would have to trust that I was being honest.

All the dominos would fall either for or against me that Saturday afternoon. If anything went wrong, I would be held responsible. I knew I was risking my job, maybe even my career. But I also knew I could not wait for them to decide to give me an opportunity. I waited nervously as family and friends, who had received a text message, waited patiently at home. Suddenly, there it was, my first-ever sports report on TV was airing nationally. I was filled with joy. The text messages were pouring in, and I felt like it was the beginning of something beautiful in my career. In a matter of seconds, I felt my life had changed, and my confidence was through the roof. Martino's interview, which I had also edited and worked on, had aired on the English side. When the producer and announcers finished with their broadcast, they congratulated me on a job well done. In that moment, I felt I had finally arrived, and the only way to go from there was up.

I felt stronger and ready for whatever came next. I thought it was a matter of time before I got a shot at different projects. I kept working on my craft every night, saving my tapes, and showing them to some of the announcers. Everything was going well and some of the announcers were paying more attention to me.

A color analyst told me that if I really wanted to do this, to keep going without looking back, regardless of the challenges ahead. Looking back, I should have seen his words as the warning they were. Just weeks after airing my report, my schedule began to change constantly, and I was always under supervision. No one had to say anything for me to know someone was purposely messing with me. This was retaliation for airing my interview.

Downward Spiral

The only thing tragedy gives us is the opportunity to rebuild our life. — Paulo Coelho

I had overcome the streets of South Central, but the corporate world was a different kind of cruel. My actions, no matter how justified, with the Chivas U.S.A. project made me a target of the producers and other leaders at Zorro. After two years of dedicated work at Zorro, I was told that there was no possibility to become an on-air reporter or play-by-play announcer. In addition, my production assignments were monitored to ensure that I couldn't get closer to being in front of the camera. I grew unhappier by the day and knew my time at Zorro was coming to an end.

In 2010, I was laid off, only months after airing that first report on TV.

A few days later, my college girlfriend of three years, Elaine, broke up with me.

Elaine was my first love. She was the woman I thought I would marry and start a family with. Elaine had become a part of my family, and everyone who met her thought she was the one for me.

My aunts and uncles had already been married or had kids by the time they were my age. They all believed I was late to the party and that I needed to start thinking about a family soon. My cousins Josue and Noe already had kids and had begun their own families. It was everything I hoped to accomplish with Elaine.

In my last year with Zorro, we had grown apart, and we realized we wanted different things out of life. I was committed to making it on TV while she wanted to explore the world. The impact of Elaine's decision to call it quits was compounded by the timing of my layoff. It was a difficult time.

Not long after the layoff and break-up, child services would remove my niece from our home. She was Ingrid's daughter and having her in our home was a stabilizing force. With my sister's long struggle with drugs and alcohol, it gave our family a way to connect and care for her daughter in a way we were never able to for Ingrid. My niece was full of life and reminded me so much of my younger sister. The removal of my niece was a devastating experience for the entire family.

I had never experienced so much loss all at the same time. At twenty-five, it felt like my life was over. I grieved for a job that had been moving me closer to my purpose, for the love and support system I lost with Elaine, and for the trauma of my niece's removal. Everything I loved was falling away from me, and I felt lost.

I looked for support from two friends who had always been uplifting and cheered for my success.

Ofelia and I met at CSUN while taking Central American studies classes together. When we weren't in class, we spent hours talking about life while drinking coffee. Ofelia was also a first-generation Salvadoran American looking to change the narrative in her family. She was smart and brutally honest when sharing what was on her mind, especially when giving me feedback on my crazy ideas.

Ofelia was a risk-taker and went after what she wanted. She constantly reminded me to do the same. Ofelia reminded me that now wasn't the time to stop believing in myself and became a positive voice in a time of distress.

Angelina and I were introduced through a mutual friend who insisted I had to get to know her for mentorship while at Zorro. She understood the toxic, competitive culture of the station and offered me real feedback on things I could control in my professional environment. Angelina had come to the U.S. as a young girl from El Salvador and was thriving in the Public Relations field. She was often the only Latina within the different companies she worked for. We had candid conversations about the industry, and I learned a lot from her about navigating tricky politics.

The girls and I met weekly at different coffee shops all around Los Angeles. We shared stories about our families and what we thought the future would look like. Angelina was going through a divorce, and it was taking a toll on her. Through our coffee meetups, she reaffirmed her optimism and her decision to start a new life without her significant other. Her work ethic was contagious and inspired me to do what was needed to succeed in anything.

Having the girls in my life kept me from completely falling apart, but I still struggled to get focused on my ambitions. Instead, I filled as much of my time as I could with anything that would distract me from my problems. The more active I stayed, the less time I thought about my niece and ex-girlfriend. I stayed busy as a way of coping with everything else that was happening in my life.

Despite alcohol being a central cause of so much pain for my family, I began to turn to drinking and other diversions to avoid painful realities. I lacked direction and started to dabble in other areas of work to make some money. I started DJing and personal training. I also became a major party animal on the weekends. This was my version of numbing what I truly felt inside.

Throughout my childhood, I had seen firsthand how drinking could lead to decisions that changed the trajectory of your life. That stayed in the back of my mind and kept me from letting alcohol take over completely. However, as a heavy social drinker, I was starting to make poor decisions that definitely had consequences.

My wake-up call came when I took a trip to South Africa to attend the 2010 FIFA World Cup. It was meant to be a trip with friends, but through networking, I connected with a small magazine called Latino Sports 360 that circulated in Colombia. I was offered the opportunity to write about my experiences while in South Africa.

It was a dream come true to work for an outlet providing World Cup coverage. The magazine had no money to pay me, but after thinking it over, I realized that I had more to gain by doing it than walking away. I was grateful for the experience that would pad my resume. Working with Latino Sports 360 would allow me to be published internationally. It was the spark I needed to get excited about my career again.

My very first night in Johannesburg, South Africa, I almost squandered my opportunity to cover the World Cup by making bad decisions with alcohol. The hostel my friends and I were staying in hosted a BBQ for all its guests in celebration of the global event. Soon after we ate and had a few drinks, the other soccer aficionados began to turn into their rooms for the night. Guests from around the world wanted to make the most of their time in South Africa and wanted a good night's rest for a fresh start the next day.

My own group urged me to stop drinking and come back to the room with them. We had an early flight to Cape Town the next morning to start our tour of the stadiums and events. I declined the offer and instead proceeded with an aggressive drinking game with a group from Germany. I drank until the early hours of the morning with a man three times my size.

I was so intoxicated that the next morning my friends were unable to wake me for our flight. I woke up in the care of the family that owned the hostel with a note that read "Meet us in Cape Town, *pendejo*" — dummy.

I missed my first flight to Cape Town and was completely alone in a foreign country. I wasted an entire day of work to find another flight. Flights were packed and hard to find, but I was able to find a spot on the last flight out for the day. I paid a lot of money to catch up with the rest of the group.

My time spent alone in the airport was the perfect opportunity to review my poor decision-making. I asked myself what I was doing with my life? I remembered myself just a few months earlier as a hungry young journalist at Zorro. How far had I fallen? I felt constricted and heavy, like a caged bird with clipped wings. I was wasting my potential and I needed to get back to myself.

I thought about who I wanted to become. The time alone reminded me how dangerous alcohol could be and I was determined not to blow any chances that could open other doors for me down the line. I held myself accountable for my actions and knew I could make other choices, better choices for my future.

The flight was a chance for a fresh start to do what I had originally intended while in South Africa. I wrote on the plane and in our hostel room alone while waiting for my friends to return from their activities in Cape Town. My friends returned to find me quietly wrapping up my first article on my laptop. My anger at myself for drinking too much and at them for leaving me behind had subsided on the plane. I was focused and ready to get to know South Africa better.

As we explored the beauty of the country, I rekindled my passion for sports journalism. I found it on top of Table Mountain, in the pulsing crowd at Cape Town Stadium during the Germany vs. Argentina match, and in the vineyards of Stellenbosch. The sound of the vuvuzelas, an instrument sounding similar to a kazoo and a staple of South African soccer, was everywhere. Each of the ten South African stadiums buzzed with the noise from the instrument. The World Cup atmosphere was electric, and my mistake the first day was ultimately erased. I was immediately re-energized.

While I felt refocused, life didn't hesitate to test my newfound resolve. There was limited Wi-Fi and the ability to search the web for research or send emails was difficult. I had to take extra steps each day in order to meet deadlines, including waking up earlier than the group to use the internet at nearby coffee shops and taking notes for stories throughout the day. Despite this, God guided my perspective, using my surroundings to strengthen my commitment.

My exploration of neighborhoods in search of Wi-Fi empowered me to see South Africa beyond the soccer stadiums. I witnessed young boys playing soccer on dirt fields resembling the ones I grew up playing on in Los Angeles. While I couldn't help but notice the similarities, I also saw the differences. Many of the children playing had no shoes on, a luxury that, no matter how poor we were in South Central, my sisters and I always had. I observed entire families walking barefoot along the side of the road during the late hours of the night. Locals would wait outside of restaurants for a chance to ask tourists for food instead of money.

Watching kids with no shoes smile and laugh as they chased after the ball made me realize my problems were small and could be overcome. It reminded me to find joy in every moment. It brought me back to my love of the game in a way that watching the professionals play could not. It was a highlight of my trip.

South Africa was also a reminder of my privilege, despite humble beginnings. Being born in a country like the United States afforded me options that a good majority of the world would never have. Those possibilities were the driving reasons my own family had left El Salvador. I was humbled and grateful for the experience.

Apartheid ended in South Africa in the 1990s, only two decades before the World Cup. It was apparent how much the country still needed to do to end racial discrimination. Although the country was no longer segregated, Black people in South Africa still faced day-to-day injustices and microaggressions. Black people were still looked at as inferior, and the legacy of racism was easily felt in the country's culture.

My experience in South Africa left me appreciative of all the things God had given me. I was able to travel to another country all the way across the Atlantic Ocean, something that no one in my family had done before. I had arrived in South Africa thinking I would spend all my time enjoying soccer and parties, an escape from home, but instead, I was gifted with an entirely different perspective about life.

I returned home a different man. I was ready to remove the distractions and face my problems. I was inspired and enthusiastic about my job search for a full-time opportunity in sports.

Out of Hardship Comes Strength

Strength does not come from winning. Your struggles develop your strength.
— Mahatma Gandhi

I returned to Los Angeles to my family's pending child custody case for my niece, Yamileth. We were all terrified about the thoughts of Yamileth being adopted by someone else. My mother's legal status meant that she couldn't take custody of Yamileth, meaning the most apt person to fulfill the role was me. So, in the middle of my job search, I took on the fight for custody of my niece.

I had realized that there weren't many opportunities in L.A. that would allow me to advance my career. This was something that I had to seriously consider as I faced taking on the responsibilities of a parent. During the custody battle, Yamileth was still staying in foster care. We had brief visits with her, but we were always required to take her back to her foster family until the case was decided. One Saturday, shortly after I returned from my trip, I drove Yamileth back to her foster care. She giggled from the backseat, listening to me sing and talk to her. She had so much joy inside of her, yet you could still see the pain in her eyes.

As a two-year-old, Yamileth did not know what was happening, but she understood the separation from all of us. It was a lot for her to be moved from place to place and between different caregivers. There was chaos around her. Watching her from the rearview mirror, with the motivation from my South Africa trip drumming within me, I knew I was making the right decision for her and my family. I also knew that once the court case was over, I would need to leave Los Angeles for an opportunity that suited my career goals.

Days after I made that decision in the car, I told my mother that once my niece's custody case was decided, I would leave Los Angeles. She cried but gave me her blessing. My mother wanted to see me fulfill my dreams. With her support locked in, I was ready to travel anywhere that would give me my next big shot.

Starting All Over Again

As long as you're still alive, you always have the chance to start again.
–Emily Acker

The media loves free work, especially startup companies that can't afford to hire actual employees. Getting custody of Yamileth was going to be a long, arduous process, and in the meantime, I needed to get myself experience in my professional field. Free work was a way for me to get into the sports scene in Los Angeles. I put my networking skills into action and called everyone who could point me toward potential work.

Through my cold calling, I was introduced to Rero, the only person open to my offer to work for free in exchange for some experience. Rero was a seasoned veteran in the sports world who had started his own project. He was creating a digital sports site during a time when online platforms were gaining popularity. Rero had the credentials and the experience to make it work.

During my job search, Rero took me on as an unpaid intern, and in return, I would learn from a guy with over twenty years in the game. My new gig suddenly gave me access to games I would have never been able to get into on my own. This was a match made in heaven.

I was determined to get back on track and open to learning more about the industry. Rero took me under his wing and began teaching me a lot I didn't know about sports reporting. He taught me basic things like where to stand inside locker rooms and how to ask tough questions most reporters weren't willing to ask. Rero taught me to show up as a professional and not as a fan. He coached me on how to best interview athletes.

I was learning skills that could only be obtained with real-life experience. I paid attention to the way Rero put together his questions and how he snuck in questions to top athletes in a room with twenty other reporters next to him. Rero walked me through every step like a master does with an apprentice.

I treated the opportunity as a full-time job. I took advantage of each prospect I had working for Rero's new sports site. This included the chance to be close to some of the best sports reporters in the city. I was able to network and ask questions of people I admired. I readopted the approach that helped me grow at Zorro to become the young professional I was, always insisting on getting some type of feedback when the opportunity presented itself. No one was going to outwork me, and my eagerness allowed me to take in everything I learned.

I had turned my layoff into an assignment that had me interviewing David Beckham, Landon Donovan, Kobe Bryant, and some of L.A.'s biggest stars within a year.

I prepared for interviews in the early mornings at local coffee shops and then either headed out to my next interview or to child services and court meetings for custody of Yamileth. It was challenging to switch in between the highs and lows of my life, from interviewing top athletes to enduring painfully long and emotional hearings.

My dedication would pay off when Rero made me an official reporter. I became his number one apprentice, and that meant I got priority when it was time to cover all events. It was recognition for all the hard work I was putting in. My new position allowed me to cover the 2011 MLS final between the Los Angeles Galaxy and the Houston Dynamo, the biggest game I had ever covered in my career. On game day, I took the extra initiative to find a camera and produce a story on video.

Grit

Don't be afraid to fail. Be afraid not to try. — Michael Jordan

After my time with Rero, I applied to over 100 TV stations around the country in the span of two years. I emailed YouTube links to my demo reel and mailed envelopes with DVD demos along with a resume to any opening I came across online.

I was willing to go anywhere, including cities that I couldn't pronounce, to get on camera and report on the latest news in sports. I wanted to be able to say that I had given sports journalism my best shot before I even considered moving on. Despite my daily hours of effort, I didn't receive many responses to my emails.

In this painful process of waiting, I added layers to my already thick skin. I became immune to rejections and would not allow the word "no" to affect me. I used the silence from stations to find motivation and kept going. I had nothing to lose when sending my demo and resume to a job opening. I stayed positive by focusing on my family and the work.

During this time, I reached out to my college friend, Jahmai Webster, who was already working in sports. He had moved from Los Angeles to Waco, Texas, and was currently working in Hawaii. Jahmai and I picked up where we had left off. Just like our time in Manzanita Hall, Jahmai reminded me to look beyond my, sometimes narrow, point of concentration. He had been the one to push me to expand beyond expertise in soccer and was encouraging me, once again, to look beyond the rejections and silence piling up.

This time Jahmai said, "All you need is one door." True to Jahmai form, his advice showed up at the right time for me, and I continued my search, only in need of one opportunity.

I printed Jahmai's advice and placed it on my wall to read when I woke up and when I went to bed. The message reminded me that I had experienced worse things and was still here. I was always able to get back up. It incentivized my persistence, even when I didn't have a clear picture of what would take place next.

Preparation, Heartache, and Lessons

Failing to prepare is preparing to fail. — John Wooden

Weeks into my relentless search process, I finally received a phone call from a news director in El Paso, Texas. He was interested in getting to know me a little better and we scheduled a series of phone conversations.

The director asked me for a current in-studio demo reel. Without access to Zorro's equipment and no longer in school, this reel was going to be more challenging to produce on my own. Luckily, my consistent connections with my journalism professor, Professor Lincoln, allowed me to reach out and request some studio time on campus. Professor Lincoln accepted and I completed a basic demo back in Manzanita Hall.

I used the reel to show my versatility by including soccer, NBA, and NFL highlights. I spoke about the Los Angeles Galaxy and the Spanish team, FC Barcelona, coming to the U.S. on tour. I reported on the NBA lockout of 2012 and Peyton Manning's recovery after having neck surgery. I emailed the director my completed demo, and a few days later, I had a plane ticket to the border town of El Paso, Texas.

I naively thought that flying to Texas also meant the job was mine. I believed I was just flying in to sign a contract. I landed in El Paso and met the news director I had been in contact with at the airport. He drove me around town and pointed out key attractions in the small border city that I thought would become my new home.

When we arrived at the station, I was introduced to the team and learned more about the organization. The director and I moved to his office, where I heard more about past sports anchors who had worked there and had moved on to jobs in bigger markets. The director also mentioned that the position they were hiring for required a two-year contract.

I sat in his office, already signing the deal in my mind. I started to daydream about the next market I would move into, just like the station's reporters he just mentioned. My mental reels didn't last long, however, because the director ended his speech with instructions to get ready for my audition. The director wanted to have something live on tape before making a final decision.

My stomach dropped and, suddenly, the room got big. I wasn't expecting to audition, and I wasn't prepared. I kicked myself because I realized I should've been ready. In front of the camera, with my body pulsing from anxious nerves, I stood to give a live commentary in front of the station's anchors, producers, and the vice president of the company, sitting comfortably behind a glass mirror inside the control room. Right out of the gate, I stumbled and mispronounced simple words and names. If this was a race, it was already over.

I made multiple mistakes that led the news director to request I start the entire segment over several times. He interrupted me a few times to do this, which only increased my angst. I choked. As we wrapped up the painful audition, I glanced over at the glass-enclosed control room to see a room full of disappointed reporters and anchors.

I finished my interview in the director's office reviewing my tape. His tone had changed from hopeful to frustration and even anger at some points. He told me that he had expected more from me after watching the comprehensive reel I had sent prior to my trip. I wanted to be swallowed up by the ground. I had blown the opportunity I had been working so hard for over the past couple of years. I left the director's office with him, concluding that they would let me know. Weeks later, I, unsurprisingly, was informed I didn't get the job.

Twenty-four hours in El Paso taught me that it is always better to be over-prepared.

Open Doors

Opportunities multiply as they are seized. — Colin Wilson

I returned to Los Angeles disappointed in my performance but optimistic about what would happen next. I just needed to make the proper adjustments to be ready for whatever chance would come.

The first adjustment on my list was to improve my teleprompter reading. I had no experience reading a screen on camera and needed to get better fast. The teleprompter would prove to be one of my biggest challenges at the beginning of my career as a studio anchor. I practiced a few times a week with the mantra that I would be prepared when another audition presented itself. I would be better the second time around.

My teleprompter practice was taking place as Yamileth's custody case was ending. My sister Karla and I would end up adopting Yamileth and keeping her safe within our family. No matter what hurdles I was jumping over in my professional life, family always came first. My mother had put me and my siblings first when she worked hard to provide for us and encouraged us to succeed in school. She put me first in my decision to pursue college and made peace with my potential move from Los Angeles.

I wanted to show up for Yamileth so that she could do the same for someone else one day. I wanted her to feel loved and have a stable home environment. I wanted her to have the opportunity to pursue her own dreams and perhaps go to college.

With the case settled, I could fully concentrate on my career. What happened next was nothing less than a miracle. The silence I had endured from stations for months suddenly turned into conversations with station directors and multiple offers. God's timing is always right, and I felt that He had removed all distractions in my personal life to concentrate on my big break. I was ready.

I got calls from McAllen and Sacramento, small to medium-sized TV markets, willing to give me a chance as a reporter. Even El Paso contacted me again with another chance to come on board as their second sports reporter.

The salary offered from the El Paso station had been reduced almost in half, going from an annual $40,000 earned to a mere $27,000 salary. After conversations with McAllen and Sacramento didn't seem any more promising, I understood that this was the only sports job on the table for me. I accepted an offer to return to the same station where I had learned an invaluable lesson in preparation.

Less than an hour after I hung up with El Paso to plan my travel back down to the station, I received a call from a company called ZGS in Washington, D.C. The station was contacting me about a demo I had sent months prior; one of the hundreds of applications I submitted but never confirmed receipt of the tape.

The ZGS news director, Dougie, informed me he had received my application along with my demo reel. He was calling all potential candidates to fill a sports position they had available. Dougie asked me questions about where my family was from and was interested in knowing more about my Salvadoran background. He wanted to know how informed I was about the Salvadoran community.

It was the first time anyone in the media asked about my background. In fact, on more than one occasion, they had advised me to lose any Salvadoran accent because it would be off-putting in the Los Angeles market that heavily favored the Mexican community.

I worked hard to remove any of the Salvadoran terms I had picked up from my vocabulary. I learned from my former Central American colleagues that I had to be as neutral as possible in my speech to be considered for the types of roles I wanted. I got rid of words like *vos* — you — and used the Mexican terms instead. I studied Colombian and Mexican reporters I knew, looking for nuances to add to my speech.

It took me a couple of years, but I was eventually able to hide my identity in language so well that people had no idea where I was from. In the D.C., Maryland, Virginia area — DMV — the desire for Central American representation was the complete opposite. This part of the country has the second-highest concentration of people from El Salvador in the U.S. The Spanish TV market in the DMV catered to the Salvadoran viewer. It's the only market in the U.S. where this is true. It was the perfect opportunity for a Salvadoran American reporter like myself trying to break into the industry.

When it was time to end the call, Dougie told me he liked what he had heard and would consider me for the job. He had a few others on his list to call, but he would get back to me in the near future. I politely thanked him for the consideration but told him I was going to decline any offers because I had a verbal agreement with the station in El Paso.

I couldn't afford to risk that job to simply be considered for another. Dougie asked if I had signed any documents yet and my answer was no. Relieved, Dougie told me to hold off on signing anything and that he would get back to me as soon as possible after a conversation with his general manager. Dougie called three days later and offered me my first full-time TV job as sports anchor.

I was shocked. Moving to the nation's capital to work in a heavily saturated Salvadoran market was a big deal. Dougie understood that I lacked live TV experience but said he was willing to work with me. More than anything, he loved the fact that I was a one-man band. I had experience editing, writing and could produce an entire segment alone. All the things I was the least passionate about were now the tools giving me my full-time time opportunity on TV news.

When asked about salary, I told Dougie the original amount offered from the El Paso station — $40,000. My lack of experience prevented me from researching the going rate in the market, as well as the cost of living in that area of the country. I had no idea what life in the DMV would cost, and not being informed would have consequences.

The salary I requested was about $20,000 to $30,000 short of an average salary in the Washington D.C. market. Dougie immediately accepted my request, and he told me he would email me the final paperwork to sign to make this job official.

I called Texas to decline my offer, making the best decision for me. D.C. had professional teams and was offering more money. I was traveling much further from home but was thrilled with the opportunities Washington D.C. offered. It was the right trade-off, and I was eager to start.

Leaving Los Angeles

We need to struggle in life to learn about ourselves. To believe in ourselves.
— Teddy Atlas

Leaving Los Angeles meant leaving my mother, my sisters, and my niece behind. In so many ways, they had come to depend on me as the man of the house. More than that, I found it hard to come to terms with leaving a group of women alone in a bad neighborhood. The decision to leave L.A. in search of the right opportunity was proving to be more difficult once I completed the final paperwork for the job. I had never lived on my own nor lived anywhere outside of Los Angeles.

I pulled strength from remembering inspiration from legendary boxing trainer Teddy Atlas. He said that, in life, you need to struggle to learn about yourself. It is the struggle that helps you believe in yourself when you're questioning whether or not you can accomplish what you set out to do. That's the moment you realize what you're able to overcome and how far you can go.

I was twenty-seven years old when I left the hood behind for Washington D.C. I would no longer need to look over my shoulder. I was free of fear from drive-by shootings, drug dealers, or gang bangers waiting in front of the building.

The move to Washington D.C. was an opportunity to change many of the stigmas that surround people of color in low-income neighborhoods. It was the chance to show the world that people who came from neighborhoods like South Central could accomplish more than what the hood had to offer. Unlike the only dream-bigger story told to many Black and Brown boys, I didn't have to be a professional athlete to be someone and strive beyond the block.

I found comfort and strength in the journey my family had taken three decades earlier. If they could travel almost three thousand miles on buses, trains, and on foot, I could make the sacrifice of being away from loved ones to reach higher.

I loved Los Angeles the same way my family loved El Salvador. These places were our homes. Leaving Los Angeles was the end of a chapter and the beginning of something that offered hope Los Angeles couldn't provide.

Taking a Risk

If you've ever gambled, you know that to win big, you have to bet big. Heading to Washington, D.C. meant selling everything I had to finance my trip and sustain myself for the first couple of months. I had just enough money to pay for the things I needed in this new start. With very few things left to my name, I packed six ties, four coats, three suits, and a TV. That was everything I owned.

Through the backdoor leading into a parking lot, I left my mom's apartment in the early morning. I paused and took a final deep breath. I made Los Angeles a promise that I would return to my city as an accomplished professional.

Josue, a good friend from college, was waiting for me in the parking lot and would join me on a cross-country road trip. As we got on the road, Josue and I remembered the times I stayed at his place until 3am to finish editing videos. The trip allowed us to bond and talk about my plans once I arrived in the capital.

We drove through Phoenix, El Paso, Amarillo, Oklahoma City, and Memphis. To save money, we slept in a rest area on our first night. Filled with anxiety, we hardly slept. Next, we tried napping in Oklahoma City inside a movie theater. The rest was not much better. The road trip was mentally and physically draining, but after two days and twelve hours, we arrived in the state of Maryland. Josue stayed with me a week after the road trip before flying back to California. It was helpful to have a familiar face in a new place.

In Maryland, I would stay with my childhood friend Chris' family for a few weeks as I got settled.
I wasted little time figuring out the landscape of Bowie, Maryland. Far from the tall buildings and traffic back in Los Angeles, Bowie was quiet, with very few things happening around town. Despite getting lost and having difficulty getting used to being away from my family, something about the peacefulness of the small town allowed me to focus and prepare before starting my new job.

186

On my first day, I drove forty-five minutes from Bowie, Maryland, to Arlington, Virginia, to meet Dougie in the lobby of the station. Similar to my interview in El Paso, Dougie showed me around the building and introduced me to my new colleagues. The station wasn't exactly what I pictured. It was a tiny place on the first floor of a big building. It really didn't look or feel like a space for newscast production. The reality of the space versus the appearance of "bigger and better" on-screen would later be a great lesson in TV magic.

Dougie and I discussed the expectations and responsibilities of my new role. I would not be on air during my first week so that I could get a feel for the workflow. In my first few days at the station, I would focus on working closely with the production team to record taped segments. These segments would not be aired and would serve as practice to get me ready.

Others on the team expected me to start right away, and the extra time Dougie gave me to practice caused others to resent me. I was greeted with passive aggression and side comments from a few co-workers. I knew this job wasn't going to be easy and that I would have to earn everyone's respect with hard work. I also knew from my time at Zorro that I was capable.

One colleague, in particular, made my start at ZGS particularly more challenging. Mr. Charpio, a producer with an Erik Estrada-like ego, was stuck in the past and often compared our work to the good old days when reporters and anchors knew how to work. He wasted little time in telling me how insufficient my performance was in comparison to previous anchors at ZGS. His criticisms chipped at my confidence, and I found myself repeating the mistakes of my El Paso interview during my first segment practice.

I practiced over and over again, but by midweek, Mr. Charpio stopped me in the middle of the segment to shout with profanity that I was inexperienced and incapable of being a professional. After a five-minute tongue lashing, I was released for a dinner break and headed to my car fighting back tears. I was frustrated.

This cycle went on for days. I used my breaks to speak with mentors, friends, and quiet time to reflect on how I could eliminate my mistakes and deliver a clear segment. I tackled my mistakes one day at a time, walking in each day ready to correct the errors of the previous practice. I discovered that in journalism, you were not afforded the luxury to sulk in the problems of yesterday. Working in TV, you had to move on and do it quickly.

I was learning to move on but was frequently interrupted by Mr. Chapiro's negative energy. When the time came for my first live segment, Dougie suggested I take a bit more time to practice and allowed me to do a voice-over for the live footage. The extra time Dougie gave me allowed me to practice with the teleprompter and conquer my fears.

I would eventually make it on TV, reporting live segments. However, I still had a lot of work to do. My talent was still raw, and I had a long way to go to become the anchor I had imagined from childhood. Feedback online also reflected that I was stiff on camera. As fall became winter, my confidence grew with the teleprompter. Mastering one element of the job allowed me to move on to finding my identity and voice as an anchor. It was time to find ways to make my light-hearted, passionate nature appear on screen.

A Guiding Voice to Journalists

Surround yourself only with people who are going to lift you higher.
— Oprah Winfrey

My luck lifted the day I met Lori Montenegro, a hard-news journalist I had only ever seen on TV. Lori was a straight shooter and told you exactly how things were without sugar-coating anything. In our very first meeting, Lori admitted she had been watching me. She placed her hand on my left shoulder and listed a few things I needed to do to improve my on-air performance. Her shortlist of tips concluded with her ability to see just how nervous I was reading the teleprompter on live TV.

I had learned before arriving in D.C., it was important to stay close to people with more experience, as well as those who had

my best interests at heart. Even one person could make a world of difference, and Lori became that person for me. She gave me expert advice and always reminded me that I knew what I was doing. Lori gave me the boost of confidence I needed to trust myself and my preparation before each segment.

Over the course of the next eighteen months, Lori would serve as a mentor to me. She checked in weekly, and we went over things I still needed to improve upon, as well as celebrated skills I had mastered. Time moved quickly, and I realized I had come to the end of the timeframe I had originally set for myself to leave D.C. I was

189

ready to search for a different opportunity in another city and shared this with Lori.

Almost instantly, Lori put an end to the idea that I was ready to leave. Rather than tell me I was still underprepared, Lori asked me to meet her during a weekend. I showed up at the station to find other anchors, a producer, and a cameraman present at Lori's request. She said we were all meeting so that I could receive feedback from people who had been in the business for years. My only responsibility was to gather all my material for everyone to review.

I received a tremendous amount of feedback that day. My peers observed that I never moved my hands. It appeared like they were stuck to the anchor desk. Others noticed how robotic I looked on camera, never turning my face to speak with my fellow

anchors. I spoke fast without pausing in between sentences. I read the teleprompter in one tone, without any emphasis on words or phrases like anyone would in a normal conversation. Instead, I stayed in a high pitch, which made me sound as if my energy was always at 200%.

Finally, I heard how distracting my colorful wardrobe was for TV. It was suggested to remove all pinks and yellows from my shirt and tie selection. The final verdict from Lori's experienced team was that I still needed time to develop in my career. I had learned and grown a lot over a period of almost two years, but I still had not learned everything ZGS had to teach me. I needed to stay.

Put in the Work

Put in the work. — Lori Montenegro

It was time to get back to basics. That meant focusing on the small details that made me better on camera during live shows. I started practicing live shots in front of the mirror again, which made a world of difference. This loosened me up before I went on air, and it was the exact same exercise professors at CSUN had recommended while I was in college.

I started staying after hours to practice at the studio once again, like I did while at Zorro. Working on things for ZGS in the ZGS space made the most sense. I went through the checklist of suggestions from Lori's expert team. First, I worked on my hand movements and tried to use them in my reporting as naturally as possible. I practiced moving my body as if to speak to my colleagues seated at the anchor desk with me. I used "rollercoaster" techniques to change my pitch in reading to make my reporting more interesting and easier to listen to. I followed every piece of advice that was given to me by the professionals.

My first ever sports promo shot and recorded by Omar García.

I also developed a system to test myself while on live TV. It was not uncommon for things in the station to stop working, including the teleprompter. I wanted to always be ready to improvise. I would begin my live segments reading from the prompter and then switch quickly to using my printed scripts in the middle of a story as seamlessly as possible. It was a risky move, but it helped me learn how to react in real-time and to stay ready with a Plan B.

On Saturdays and Sundays, I would practice reporting from the field, which meant interviewing people and athletes on camera. It was the perfect time to interact with a community that was only beginning to know my name. I was, however, still making mistakes, which would catch people off guard and cause the bystander crowd to roar with laughter. There was more vulnerability being on camera in front of live crowds.

Without the safety of the studio on the weekends, I learned how to turn the noise off. I learned to see past all the people staring at me and focus solely on my work. It didn't matter who was watching, how many people were there, or what their reaction was when I messed up. I just kept going. People would shout my name or walk right in front of the camera to get my attention. During live games, highly intoxicated fans would yell at the camera.

Sometimes I would be on camera with crowds of more than fifty people behind me. I wouldn't leave until the job was finished, which sometimes meant I needed to repeat myself multiple times. I realized that if I could control a crowd of people, I could do anything. It was all part of the show and the lessons I was learning.

Lori's mantra of "put in the work" replayed for me during the most challenging of times. It kept me going to overcome my shortcomings. It meant being the first to arrive and the last to leave. It meant keeping my head down to finish a job and ignoring chatter on social media. Months later, putting in the work showed a recognizable difference. I was beginning to flow on camera.

I was inspired to improve. I no longer needed extra motivation to keep going. There was a fire in me that no longer needed fuel to burn. Los Angeles media folks call this being a lion in the business.

Attitude of a Lion

I don't care if you're a gazelle or a lion when the sun is up! You better get to running! — Eric Thomas

What does it mean to be a lion versus a gazelle? Friends and mentors in Los Angeles would often ask me which animal I would rather be, and I never quite understood what they meant until my interactions with Lori. They were asking me if I would rather be motivated or inspired.

At the beginning of my journey, I was motivated by the desire to prove to people that I belonged. Much like the gazelle, running to avoid danger, something external had always fueled me to keep going.

Gazelles only run fast when threatened. Gangs and poverty were all external hazards. Even soccer, to some degree, had been an outside motivator to fit in and ensure I could play to avoid gang culture. I had been running my entire childhood just to survive. While they had all been helpful in getting me to accomplish my goals, those motivators meant that my objectives were always a means to an end. In my eyes, my achievements would get me out of the hood, provide for my family, or just prove everyone wrong.

With the help of Lori and her expert team, something shifted for me in D.C. I was no longer reacting to a force outside myself. There was an internal desire to get better. I no longer saw my success for what I could get out of but what I could do with it and the joy I could find in it. I was inspired. I woke up every morning with the drive to get better at each thing on my list of suggested improvements.

Lions are only successful in less than 20% of their hunts. Just like the lion, my new mindset didn't mean I thought I was stronger or better. It meant that I accepted that I would fail more often than I would succeed. But, like a lion, I would be recognized for my successes. I was ready to conquer whatever I wanted, no matter the obstacle, much like a wild lion.

The Perfect Instructor: Building Relationships, Building My Career

Omar García became a friend and mentor that helped me become a more polished journalist throughout my career.

Like Lori Montenegro, I met another person who would serve as a mentor and help me develop even further as an anchor-reporter. Omar García began working for ZGS around the same time I arrived in 2012. He was a former ESPN producer who worked shoulder to shoulder with some of the industry's biggest upcoming talent at the time.

Omar was blunt with feedback about on-camera performances. He would require talent to re-record any bad stand-ups, promos, or scripts as many times as necessary to get the perfect clip. His attitude could turn some people off. However, his responses were never personal and always related to the work. Omar knew what he was talking about.

Working next to Omar meant you were going to learn something new. Whether it was noticing your energy on camera or learning new ways to shoot a video, Omar paid attention to the smallest nuances most journalists missed. Working side by side with Omar opened my eyes to things I hadn't paid attention to in the past but were important in achieving an excellent segment. I often left our projects with a list of areas for growth.

Omar and I connected around our drive to keep getting better. While all our co-workers enjoyed their days off on the weekends, we worked on recording our next story. Omar was always willing to show me how to do things I didn't know how to do and never expected anything in return.

When Omar wasn't available on weekends, I would cover games or events on my own. I attended practices and press conferences looking to build relationships and open new doors. I traveled for events I wanted to cover, even those that were hundreds of miles away in New York City, Philadelphia, and Delaware. I went wherever I saw an opportunity to make an industry connection and put my skills to work.

I didn't always enjoy traveling or attending practices and games on the weekends, but it was an investment in my career. I was going to do something to advance my work even when I didn't feel like doing it. It was my approach to everything I did, and I knew my hard work would eventually bear fruit.

I went to different sporting events to get diversity in the games I covered. Every sport had a unique world of its own, which meant I was meeting new groups of people all the time in attempts to get interviews. It was complicated to navigate such a diversity of settings. This was especially true during the summers when European teams toured the U.S., Major League Baseball season was open, and the NFL was in training.

I continued to learn from all the other seasoned journalism professionals around me, using the analyzing skills I picked up from my time with Rero to observe their processes. No two reporters were the same, each one prepared differently. I was establishing myself in the market, while many of my predecessors at ZGS had rarely left the studio to cover events.

Omar and I during our first ever NFL coverage in Washington D.C.— the RG3 era in 2012-2013.

I was finding a niche for myself. No one before me at ZGS had ever established a relationship with the professional teams in the city. This made getting interviews more difficult. Media personnel recognized the mic flag but often mentioned that we never showed up to cover any of the games or practices. Additionally, the station's reputation wasn't great based on a few unfortunate incidents that had taken place before I was hired. I had to build relationships with local professional teams, like the Washington Nationals, Washington Wizards, Washington Football Team, and D.C. United, from the ground up.

The Washington Football Team was the hardest team to gain access to but would become the first franchise to fully open its doors to me as a journalist. I built that team relationship through consistency and professionalism. It was the boost I needed to get the ball rolling with other teams. ZGS's reputation improved with my exchanges as well. The station moved from somewhat of a media pariah to strong allies in a matter of years.

Omar and I never missed a pre or regular-season game at FedEx Field covering the NFL. Game days were opportunities to record new footage in and out of the stadium. These were stories and a sport our TV audience wasn't used to seeing. The ZGS audience was predominantly Latino and Spanish-speaking. The NFL had been trying for years to get more Latinos to watch football, and we were slowly making progress by showing the atmosphere of games in a way to ignite any sports fans' interest. Without knowing it, I was helping the station to cross cultural boundaries through sports.

Kobe Bryant's last game in Washington D.C.

When I wasn't at an NFL game, the Robert F. Kennedy Stadium, or RFK, was my second home to cover D.C. United. D.C. United was a four-time Major League Soccer champion. However, most DMV stations rarely showed the team. As a Latino journalist, D.C. United was my most important franchise. They played the sport most of my station's viewers followed — soccer. The championship days of the MLS team were a decade gone when I started covering D.C. United. Despite their standing within the league, Omar and I showed up at practice and games all season.

It wasn't important that they weren't winning. While it would have been nice for them to have some success (I remembered my glory days of covering L.A. Galaxy with Rero for two championship wins), Omar and I wanted to create something much bigger. We were looking to connect fans with the heart and soul of the team to ensure fan loyalty, regardless of the outcome. Furthermore, D.C. United's lack of popularity allowed us greater access to the team with less media competition around.

D.C. United only won three games and had the league's worst record in my second year at ZGS. They needed all the coverage they could get. I was granted access to walk freely around the stadium, record in the stands, and get as creative as I wanted with segments. This was a time of real growth for me as a field reporter. With Omar by my side, I improved my stand-ups — narration into the camera from a script, fan interactions inside of the stadium, and locker room interviews.

Choose Your Battles Wisely

Omar and I remained close and worked on numerous projects together over the years. I also started creating new content on my own. I traveled to New York City to cover boxing events, which quickly became a favorite creative outlet for me. I was in the *Big Apple* when I met Beto Duran, a selfless, hardworking sportscaster and journalist from Los Angeles, and instantly hit it off.

Beto and I met covering the same event in New York and immediately found that we had much in common. Our conversation led me to share my professional journey with Beto. He praised me for driving the four hours to New York City to cover big matches. He affirmed all the extra time I was putting in and told me to continue doing it.

I had once thought I was crazy because I was spending the little money I had to go to another city to cover boxing. I was paying to travel out-of-pocket. Beto reminded me about the power of relationships. I would meet and be seen by the people managing the events. Most of these individuals would probably never watch me on TV but would start to notice me covering their event. It might keep me top of mind for opportunities in the future.

When I returned from NYC, Dougie delivered the crushing news that they no longer wanted me to cover smaller events on weekends. I would still be allowed to cover larger events a few times per year, but that all other weekend segments should stop. I had been buzzing from Beto's feedback that I was doing the right thing, only to return to an announcement that felt like it was constricting my professional progress.

Dougie had major budget concerns. The almost non-existent sports department didn't have the funds to pay for the work on weekends. While I didn't mind doing the work for free, other co-workers were feeling pressure to work on weekends as well and wanted to be paid. By asking Omar to come along, problems mounted because he wasn't officially a part of our department.

Dougie was starting to worry about conflicts with other departments as well.

I pleaded with Dougie, reminding him that so much of our work in sports happened on the weekends. I wanted to remain consistent with our viewer base that had started to rely on our in-person, real-time coverage of sports around D.C. But the answer was still a no, and I was left feeling like I had been invited into a fight with both hands tied behind my back.

I thought back to the Chivas U.S.A project back at Zorro. I remembered feeling the same disappointment and restriction when they denied me that opportunity. I was still learning to respect the hierarchy while working for a large media company. This was an important lesson in my career for many reasons. I hadn't done myself any favors by going against my higher-ups in a less than honest way at Zorro. As unfair as it felt, their decisions were based on more people than just me. In order to move up and have better opportunities, I needed to be well-liked so that I could be considered for things outside my day-to-day job. This meant learning how to follow orders even when I didn't agree with them.

It would take a few stumbles before I bought into the concept of picking and choosing my battles. Like I often did when things weren't working out the way I expected, I called the people I trusted the most. They all said the same thing, *"be smart and to know when to pull back — winning every battle was impossible."*

It was clear that if I wasn't willing to follow instructions and accept the decisions made by management, I might be cutting my career short. I shifted my mindset and looked at my circumstances as another step in my development as a professional. Allowing my emotions to get the best of me would be counterproductive.

My general manager told me I had a lot of guts for speaking so directly about my concerns, but I needed to measure my words when talking to someone who had the power to fire me or make my life harder. I didn't take her advice for granted and incorporated it into my everyday demeanor at work. I thought that if the general manager was telling me this, it was for a reason.

I stopped pushing back. It wasn't getting me anywhere, and it only created more friction. My reactions to things out of my control would determine the outcomes. I learned the formula "situation + reaction = outcome." I learned to express my frustration in a more productive manner, especially as I voiced concerns with high-level management.

After a few months, things calmed down. I didn't believe, however, that the tranquility would last for a long time. I was applying to different stations around the country. I interviewed in Denver, Colorado, and Houston, Texas. I received an offer from the station in Houston but turned it down due to their inability to meet my salary request. I had come to know my worth in D.C., and I wouldn't let my mistake of accepting a significantly lower salary at ZGS happen again.

Big Apple Dreams

In the summer of 2014, I felt that something great was about to take place in my career. I received an invitation to audition in New York for a big sports league. It was an on-camera job for the online site that covered everything related to the league. This was the first time in my career I would audition for an English-speaking company.

I had prior experience doing bilingual work for a few companies back in Los Angeles and D.C., but those jobs were minor in comparison to what was before me. I had started working on a bilingual demo when Omar and I had gotten into a groove of our weekend work. Progress on the demo accelerated when ZGS banned me from covering events on weekends. This opportunity in NYC was like a dream come true.

The FIFA World Cup was taking place in Brazil, and the company planned to send a big group to cover the U.S National Team during the tournament. I was interviewing for a position on that big team. I landed at JFK airport and was greeted by a driver holding a sign with my name on it. I was thrilled and looked forward to the week of interviews ahead.

As we drove over the highways and bridges, I imagined what living in NYC would be like. The driver dropped me off in a sea of skyscrapers, and I looked up in amazement. I had been to New York a few times before to cover boxing matches, but this time felt different. I was experiencing the city in a new way. I said a prayer and walked into the station.

I passed sports memorabilia, bobbleheads, and large, framed posters lining the walls. There was a bar inside the station where employees could play video games or have a drink after work. It wasn't your typical newsroom. This was a workplace from the future, one I thought only existed in industry rumors. The place looked like a scene out of a movie.

I met the team, including the vice president of the company, in a large boardroom with more sports posters decorating the perimeter. The VP asked me how I liked the city and if I would be willing to move to New York if the position was offered. I answered that I would strongly consider it if we got to that point. Our conversation wasn't long, but it was good and informative. More importantly, he was surprised to find out that I had followed the brand since it had been launched almost two decades earlier.

Over the next four days, I met the station's talented staff and learned more about their experiences working at the company. I found the only two Latino employees working on the English side. There was a lack of diversity present, despite the company promoting inclusion in most of its marketing materials. There were less than a handful of Latinos and one Black person working for the digital side of the business. The Spanish-speaking media team was made up of one reporter and one producer. They worked in a small back room far away from the rest of the larger team.

As I noticed these details, one of my new Latino contacts warned me not to believe everything I had heard. He was born in New York City to a Honduran family and was a first-generation American, just like me. He was thrilled to see another Latino walk through their doors but was also honest about how difficult the lack of diversity could be at the station.

In addition to the inclusivity red flags I had observed, I was also shocked by how disorganized leaders in the station appeared to be. I was prepared to do anything, a lesson my audition in El Paso and first few weeks in D.C. had taught me. However, most of my time there was spent quickly catching up to an idea that was presented only minutes before. I was coming from a high-paced environment where multitasking was part of our jobs, but everything at this station seemed rushed, last minute, and sometimes sloppy.

After another exhausting day trying to understand the larger plan behind my audition, I asked my new Honduran American friend to join me for dinner. As we discussed the studio over a meal, my new friend mentioned that he didn't think my interview was being taken seriously. The station had struggled with diversity in the past, and he believed I was being entertained to show some candidates of color were given a chance.

I felt sick. Returning to the station for my final day of auditions and interviews, my horrors from the night before were confirmed. I was informed that if I were to be hired, it would be for a different role than the one I came for. I received feedback about my presence on camera being too "news-like" and even comments about a minor accent I had when reporting in English.

I was asked to be the humorous reporter for the station, covering fluff stories while my white counterparts got to work on the serious pieces of content.

For the first time in my career, I experienced discrimination based on my ethnic background. I had worked hard for this opportunity and was thrilled when I had arrived in NYC. I left the city demoralized by the industry more than by the individuals working in it. Similar to my experiences growing up in L.A., Latinos were viewed as less than capable or serious by our white neighbors.

I thanked the station's managers for their time, and I left for D.C. very angry. I knew I would not be back. I questioned my decision to audition for mainstream media. I thought about how often people of color were told or shown their places in the world and how those positions were so often less than the person's worth. I worried that this experience might be the norm for English-speaking stations.

I spoke to Beto after my NYC trip and realized I had been searching for a place in the mainstream media because that is what I thought my next step was supposed to be. Through our conversation, I discovered that working for a big station like the one in New York had requirements that I didn't want to deal with.

I was comfortable and flourishing in the Spanish market. Why did I need to leave right now? I made the decision to focus on my work in Spanish TV and nothing else for a while longer. I put my desire to be a bilingual journalist on ice for a few more years.

The Voice of D.C. United

I will never forget the memories from childhood, walking down the train tracks in south Los Angeles, doing play-by-play calls for soccer games from the 1990s. It was the moment in my life I chose to pursue a career in sports.

I was slowly achieving the dream of that 7th grader on the tracks. I had become a solid Spanish journalist.

From my networking time with Omar, an old friend and colleague contacted me to audition for the play-by-play announcer position at RFK stadium. Despite a few rough years, D.C. United was one of the most decorated soccer clubs in MLS. The team had partnered with the biggest radio station in the city. They needed an on-air personality to give the play-by-plays of the games, and my name had been thrown into the conversation.

The historic RFK stadium is where I spent every weekend during D.C. United home games for many years.

The soccer announcer position for D.C. United was highly sought after, mostly because the team was a popular franchise among the Latino community. I was an amateur compared to others auditioning for the role. Most of my experience came from announcing games at the high school and junior college level or in the recording booth at Zorro Sports.

With only a few days to prepare for a live game, I called every announcer I knew for tips and feedback. I went into overdrive doing anything possible to get ready, including researching the names of players, the team history, and other random facts associated with both teams playing.

I arrived at RFK so early I saw the security guards show up. I sat in the booth and poured my everything into the 90-minute game. It was the first professional game I announced.

The director of programming was impressed with my work, and as soon as the broadcast was over, he offered me the job. I had two jobs, one as a professional play-by-play announcer and the other as a TV sports anchor. While it meant twice the work, I gladly accepted the challenge.

There was an enormous difference between radio and TV work. As an anchor, I always had very little time to develop a sports segment. I could never surpass three and a half minutes of content most days. Radio, on the other hand, encouraged me to elaborate on points without worrying about time. I had to fill almost two and a half hours of airtime on any given Saturday. Radio was the place for me to enhance my improvising skills.

There were plenty of challenges being a play-by-play announcer. Sometimes I needed to hire a color commentator to assist me with games. This was an out-of-pocket expense for me, but I appreciated the help and the chance to give others in the area an opportunity to get into the play-by-play circle in the DMV.

Being a radio announcer gave me experience I could not gain anywhere else, and it put me on the map as a play-by-play announcer. I grew with each broadcast, learning to slow the game down in my mind. I got a better understanding of what each team was doing on the field and how to use my words to paint a better picture for the listeners.

I would announce over 100 games on the radio for D.C. United. The position allowed me to eventually cross over to announcing for the NFL. I became the official Spanish voice, one of only a few in the U.S., of the Washington Football Team just two years later.

My dedication to professional and personal growth was starting to pay dividends.

Find Your Relentlessness Again

To move into the lead means making an attack requiring fierceness and confidence, but fear must play some part in the last stage.
— Roger Bannister

With US National Team Fans before a friendly match at RFK Stadium.

In 2016, my college friend Jahmai Webster traveled to D.C. to take part in an annual journalism conference between the National Association of Hispanic Journalists and the National Association of Black Journalists. I wasn't planning to attend that year, but after some convincing from Jahmai, I agreed to go.

Jahmai said that, at best, my future job could be waiting for me at the conference, and at the very least, the convention had a number of interesting workshops I could benefit from. This conference was easily a place to run into talent from ESPN producers to national network correspondents.

It just so happened that I had decided to work on my bilingual demo again, and this seemed like the right opportunity to get feedback and share it. Within the first day, I had a few job offers based on the demo I showed. I was rebuilding my confidence after my New York humiliation.

At the conference, I ran into my old coworker and friend Joe, who suggested I speak to his friend Peter Balt, also in attendance. Peter Balt worked for ESPN and focused on their inclusion strategies. He was well known among Latino journalists who had worked with him.

Peter agreed to meet me and watch my demo reel. We sat down and he proceeded to ask me a number of questions, including my place of birth and, eventually, why all my work was in Spanish if I was clearly bilingual. It had been two years since my audition in New York, and I was just starting to be open to work in English again. I didn't share this with Peter.

Peter told me that I needed content in English. I spoke two languages, and that was an asset. Peter urged me not to limit my options and shared what others in the industry would look for in a bilingual demo reel. The conversation was a game-changer for me. I was finally ready to showcase my work in English.

The Underdog

It ain't about how hard you hit, it's about how hard you can get hit and keep moving forward. — Rocky Balboa

Since childhood, people throughout my life told me I wasn't good enough to accomplish the most basic things in life, like finishing school or staying away from drugs. It was a twisted way of thinking that plagued many people in my neighborhood. I saw that many times the cards were stacked against me, and I would have to rise up to prove others wrong. I was somewhat of an underdog.

As an adult, the messages continued that I was not good enough to move further along in my career. I was expected to stumble and quit, but I never did. Instead, I read stories about athletes who had overcome all odds and achieved the unthinkable. I figured if they could do it, so could I.

My latest challenge would be to become a bilingual journalist in the face of news directors and other reporters who told me it was impossible. There were very few fully bilingual journalists in the country.

In sports, any champion was once a contender before making it to the top. Most athletes will tell you that they were counted out before they had their big moment. When James 'Buster' Douglas took on Mike Tyson in Tokyo in 1990, no casino wanted to show the fight because they thought the investment wasn't worth it. Everyone believed Tyson, with a 37-0 winning record, would destroy Buster Douglas within the first few rounds.

The world wasn't prepared for Douglas to win anything. Douglas had great height and the perfect build but had never quite lived up to his potential. Three years earlier, Douglas had lost a title fight via technical knockout to Tony Tucker. Against Tyson, the announcers made it clear they backed Tyson, the heavy favorite and defending unified champion.

Weeks before the big fight, Douglas lost his mother, and more speculation mounted that his fight would end in failure. Before the fight, he told reporters he was coming off a great training camp, and when the bell rang, he would shock the world. Douglas went on to dominate the entire fight.

After winning round after round, Douglas surprised everyone just as he had promised. In round eight, Douglas went down after getting hit by a famous Tyson uppercut, but he got back up. In the tenth round, Douglas pounded Mike Tyson with a flurry of punches he couldn't recover from. Proving all those who had doubted him wrong, Buster Douglas was the new champion of the world.

I took stories like that of Buster Douglas to show me that if I didn't believe in myself, no one would. If I stayed ready, no matter how bad the storm was, I could handle it. A person with a powerful foundation or belief system is difficult to break, and I had taken years to build my own. I finally had my feet planted firmly on the ground, and by this point in my career, the faith I had developed in myself gave me the strength to keep working. I was no longer looking for a job. This was a search to transcend.

Qatar: Small Country, Big Dreams

In Doha Qatar in the sand dunes doing a special report on how the country was getting ready for the 2022 World Cup.

In sports, things can change in the blink of an eye. After years in my profession, I wanted to be ready for whatever came my way next. In 2010, I traveled and did some freelance reporting during the 2010 World Cup in South Africa. I hoped that I would be able to do the same for the 2014 World Cup in Brazil.

Brazil did not become a reality. Still, I kept moving and set my focus on reporting at the 2018 World Cup in Russia. I used my D.C. United play-by-play job as my training ground and the trampoline that would get me to the next big tournament. For years, I dedicated myself in mind, body, and soul to the idea that I would be chosen to cover the event.

I kept my options open to any possibility that could help me become a better journalist. At the end of 2015, I received a phone call from a colleague, Hurran, an Egyptian reporter and correspondent for some Middle Eastern news outlets. Hurran and I had always shared sports information and helped each other out during press conferences. During this phone call, Hurran extended an invitation for me to join him in Qatar with other journalists covering a popular Middle Eastern sports conference.

I had agreed to take risks in my career at this point, and this would be one of the biggest ones. The only thing anyone knew about the tiny Middle Eastern country was that it was wealthy and rich in oil. Qatar had also recently beat the United States out of hosting the 2022 World Cup, only six years away.

After a twenty-hour flight and a switch in Bahrain, I landed in Doha, Qatar's capital city. A year prior to my arrival, ESPN had made a documentary about the working conditions in the country. Security was wary of journalists and cameras. I was questioned in the airport about my equipment but shortly released to meet the rest of the journalists who had also made the trip. It was the first time I had ever taken part in anything like this outside of the U.S.

Sports reporters from different parts of the world congregated in the lobby. Everyone was looking for someone who spoke the same language in order to have a conversation. There were more than 100 of us ready to report on the sports conference ahead. I was one of four journalists attending from the U.S. and was one of the few reporters there by myself. I had no cameraman or production support.

For a period of five days, I got up early to shoot the sunrise and record b-roll footage for my report. When I wasn't recording, I was socializing with the locals and asking questions about life in Qatar.

It didn't take long for me to befriend some organizers of the event. The coordinators hoped this conference would show the world that Qatar had amended any wrongdoing many media outlets accused them of doing. They had also put together a series of panels, workshops, and discussions related to the 2022 World Cup.

Everyone's willingness to talk and showcase Qatar made it easy to coordinate interviews. I was able to interview Hassan Al Thawady, the Secretary General of the Supreme Committee for Delivery and Legacy for the World Cup, during my time there. He was the face representing Qatar to the world. I also spoke with some of the biggest media outlets in the world industry. From Diario Olé in Argentina, Marca in Spain, and L'Equipe in France, all media outlets that covered soccer religiously were present.

I gathered information for my report while meeting amazing professionals from around the globe. We visited Khalifa International Stadium together, which was still being constructed in preparation for the World Cup. I fantasized about returning in 2022 for the World Cup to see the breathtaking structure complete.

One year later, I was invited back to Qatar to cover another global sporting conference. This time I invited Omar to come along. Together, we would do something no one in the Washington D.C. area had ever done. We produced a thirty-minute show with a two-man production crew.

Initially, our intent was to produce two or three special reports about the country and sports. Thanks to connections I had built, we were given access to Qatar beyond the limits of the original show we had outlined. We knew we had to take advantage of their hospitality and changed our plans to create a much more expansive program.

Qatar was still non-existent within media coverage. The Russia 2018 World Cup was two years away and the world's attention was fixated there. Omar and I knew that, eventually, attention would shift to Qatar once the World Cup in Russia was over. This was a perfect chance for us to get a head start on programming.

With the help of my new contacts turned friends, Omar and I would explore Qatar like very few reporters had done at that point. We thought outside of the box and focused on other things aside from soccer. We were immediately led on an exclusive tour to the Sheikh's personal ranch, where some of the top camels in the Middle East were bred and trained. The facilities were worth over fifty million dollars, a price that did not include the animals. Omar and I were only the second set of cameras to be granted access to this place.

Exploring the city of Doha with locals and learning about their culture.

Omar and I had to meet a driver at a specific location and then change vehicles to begin our journey to the ranch. Security was tight. Once we arrived at the facilities, we saw a number of buildings covering a large area surrounded by rocks and desert.

Inside the gates, the facility was filled with top-dollar equipment and the best camel trainers in the world. From treadmills for animals to training pools and artificial insemination labs, the ranch was ready to produce and train the fastest camels on the planet.

Before the day's end, we watched our first-ever camel race in the middle of the desert of Al Shahaniya. Omar and I had a firsthand account of a race nothing like anything we had ever seen in our years of covering sports. American horse races had nothing on a race of camels with the open desert in the background.

Vehicles paced next to the camels on the track while camels reached speeds of up to thirty miles per hour. In these vehicles, trainers gave the animals indications through a walkie-talkie in a robot jockey placed on top of the camel's back. This would become one of the best experiences I've had as a sports reporter.

The camel race was just beginning for us. Leaving the ranch, Omar and I went on to visit Qatar's dunes. We rode four by four trucks through the sand as we looked over the beautiful blue ocean. Dune racing was an extreme sport many of the young locals and visitors practiced each winter.

We moved from camel races and dune runs to interviews with athletes, including one of the biggest soccer stars in the history of the game. Michael Laudrup, an ex-Barcelona and Real Madrid star, was now coaching a team named Al Rayyan in the Middle East. I had grown up admiring Michael Laudrup and had watched him play in the Spanish league.

Interviewing soccer legend Michael Laudrup— former FC Barcelona and Real Madrid player.

We concluded our time in Qatar with the legendary interview and left for D.C. satisfied with our work. Omar and I had just produced a show that would be a highlight of our careers and something people would talk about in the industry for years. We would go on to win an Emmy for our coverage in Qatar.

Unclear Picture

Upon our return to the States, the year would be one filled with uncertainty for me. There were loud rumors that our company was going to be sold and all of us would be laid off. The idea of the ZGS being sold created panic among the news team and raised a lot of questions that were brushed under the carpet by management. Eventually, the truth could no longer be contained, and the sale became public information.

ZGS was just a signature away from being sold for over 300 million dollars. Washington D.C. was just one of a dozen stations around the country owned by one parent company. It didn't take long before a few co-workers decided to take new jobs at different stations as soon as they were made offers. Stability was no longer a reality at ZGS.

Like my colleagues, I also sent out my resume. Unlike years prior when I searched for a job, this time, phone calls came pouring in, including one offer from Zorro Sports that could take me back home to Los Angeles. More than seven years had gone by since my time there, and the company was now under new management. I liked the idea of going back to California.

Two years earlier, an opportunity to work with the Lakers media team had been offered. I had declined because it wasn't a good fit. I would have loved to work for one of my favorite teams, but I would have had to focus solely on basketball as a behind-the-camera production member rather than a reporter. My experiences at boxing events, announcing soccer games, and my trips to Qatar would have never been possible.

This time, the offer with Zorro would allow me to both return home and keep the diversity of my coverage in sports. Listening to the offer on the phone made me feel like this could be the job I had been working towards. It was a TV opportunity at the network level. There was only one problem, it was a freelance position, and there was no guarantee that I would be employed for the long term.

I consulted with all my mentors about the offer and received mixed reviews. It was a conundrum that I would have to solve on my own.

I contemplated all of my options. If I went back home, I would be closer to my family, but I had no idea what would happen within the next year or two. If I stayed in Washington D.C., getting hired by the new company, NBC Universal, that planned to acquire ZGS was not promised. Either decision felt like a gamble, and I would have to roll the dice and see what happened.

Without much hesitation, I decided to stick with my gut and not my heart. I decided to stay in Washington D.C. It didn't feel like the right time to run. I believed in myself and was willing to stick around to see if the new changes at the station would result in bigger opportunities.

ZGS owners made it clear that only a few of us would be hired on because the new company wanted to rebrand and bring in a new team. My next few months were filled with anxiety as I waited to hear back on whether I would remain with the company. This was the nature of the business.

After a few interviews with new management, I was offered a job. It was truly an unforeseen blessing and the end of one chapter in my career and the beginning of a new one.

I took this new beginning as an opportunity to become a mainstream TV bilingual reporter. I wasn't being hired as a bilingual journalist, but I hoped to create that pathway myself.

I told the general manager, Jackie Bradford, my plans on the first day we met. I explained to Jackie that my goal was to be one of the top bilingual journalists in the country, and I was now in the perfect place with their station to make that goal a reality. Jackie responded by smiling and telling me that we would see what happened. It wasn't an immediate no, and I took that as an open door to revisit the subject when the time was right.

Time to Shine

I was speaking my goal into existence, and things would begin to move faster than expected. Three months after my conversation with Jackie, I had my make it or break it moment. I was assigned to cover a live sporting event and do coverage in both English and Spanish. For years, I had envisioned this precise moment, and though it was here, I couldn't believe it.

I was ready but knew that working in two different languages presented an entirely new set of challenges. Being able to switch languages in seconds was difficult, and I had to prepare the segment in both languages, which meant doing twice the amount of work.

At the Audi Field during the live broadcast of a D.C. United match during the MLS regular season.

In the beginning, the switch between English and Spanish made me stumble as I waited for my brain to catch up and look for the correct words in the right language. Using my past failures as motivation, I played it as safe as I could. I opted to go in and out of my live coverage to buy myself a little time to shift my thoughts and words. I had seen another journalist freeze moving between English and Spanish a few weeks earlier, and I planned to avoid his mistake.

The day after my live appearance, Jackie congratulated me for being the first to cross over to mainstream TV at the station. Jackie believed that while I had done a good job, she also knew I could do better. Over the next six months, she stayed close to me as I was assigned to different coverages. Jackie dared me to be great and not hold back.

At this time, I began my old process of sending my demos to other professionals around the country for feedback. In addition to Jackie B, I listened to other colleagues give me advice on how I could improve. I was at it again, working daily to master new skills that would allow me to be the best bilingual journalist I could be.

Drowning Out the Noise

Me versus me, no competition. — Team Don't Quit Get Fit

Reporting in English opened me up to new kinds of discrimination. One producer from a different station told me that I spoke street English, but it was okay because he knew I was raised in the hood. He said it with such ease that I knew this was not the first time for such an observation.

People asked why I was the one being sent to work games in both languages. Others believed that because I was Latino, I only knew about soccer and nothing else. Negative tweets and messages came in via social media. I ignored the comments and kept my focus on what was important, which was to do the best job possible. I wouldn't allow opinions to get under my skin. It wasn't the first time in my life someone thought I wasn't capable of doing something based on the color of my skin or where I was from.

Alongside Telemundo 44 colleagues, Alberto Pimienta and Claudia Curiel during the Washington Nationals World Series celebration.

What always kept me going was the vision of one day seeing myself as an established bilingual reporter in the country. I wanted people to see me and associate my face with two different languages. That alone gave me the energy to keep my emotions under control whenever I would hear people say cruel things. It felt as if my character was being tested, and I had to show I was the bigger person.

When I told people my family was from El Salvador, they immediately asked if I had ever been associated with the MS-13 (Mara Salvatrucha) gang. This made me upset. The comments were no longer just a personal attack on me, but on my culture and my family. We still had so much work to do as a community, city, and country. I felt responsible for doing something about it.

Crossing over to mainstream TV was like beginning to climb a mountain all over again, but one that appeared to be much steeper. I was also becoming an ambassador for my community and for those who didn't have a platform.

I shared my concerns with a close friend who advised me to put blinders on. Much like horses in a race, I needed to stay focused on the task at hand and avoid any distraction, including hurtful comments that had the potential to knock me out of emotional alignment.

I had to put my blinders on and run my race without worrying about what was said or what people thought about me. I could accomplish a lot more by being a good example and doing my best. The negative comments wouldn't disappear, but they didn't matter as much. The end goal was a lot bigger. I had the opportunity to change how Salvadorans were perceived in the United States. I had to block all negativity out and let the work do the talking for me.

It took a couple months, but before I knew it, I established the workflow of a bilingual reporter-anchor. This granted me more flexibility in the types of events I could cover. I was sent to Spring Training with the Washington Nationals to cover the MLB team in West Palm Beach, Florida. It was half a week of news reports and assignments for both stations, one after another.

I was now doing multiple hits at a time, flipping that bilingual switch with more confidence. The workload became easier to manage, and I saw every hit on the news as a chance to get better. Spring Training would turn out to be a success, mostly because I had no expectations from the trip. I was just happy to be there.

How Far I've Come from What I've Learned

Alongside JP Finlay during an interview that went viral while eating pupusas on TV.

There is a book by author Gary Bishop, in which he quoted, "Expect nothing and accept everything." These words would change the way I saw my life and career as I let go of expectations and focused only on the work directly in front of me.

I had been disappointed before, especially when I wasn't selected to join the teams covering the World Cups in Brazil and Russia. I thought I was ready, and I deserved to be a part of those teams traveling abroad. When I stopped believing I deserved things and adopted Bishop's simple phrase as a part of my work, things began to look up.

I worked diligently, without expecting anything in return. I worked without seeking a reward, praise, or more money. I just wanted to do the best job possible, which meant delivering the best bilingual content for both the stations I worked for. There were good days and bad ones, but each opportunity left me with a ton of knowledge.

At this time, sports teams in D.C. were taking off. The Capitals had reached the Stanley Cup Finals for the second time in their history. They would face the newly founded Las Vegas Knights, and I was there to cover the event. At the Stanley Cup, I would be filling in for Sherree, the main sports anchor, who was getting married.

For the Stanley Cup Finals, it was just me and my cameraman. I was in charge of every single hit in the newscast from 4pm to 7pm in both English and Spanish. I barely had enough time to catch my breath for a few seconds in between switching languages and doing the segment all over again every twenty to thirty minutes.

The Capitals went on to win their first-ever Stanley Cup Finals, and I would cover my first-ever championship parade as a reporter. It was hard to believe that months prior, I was being questioned on my knowledge of sports beyond soccer. I had proven that I was more than capable of delivering when being called upon.

Six years of working in Washington D.C. gave me more experience than I had ever imagined. I went from producing stories in countries like Qatar, Costa Rica, and Canada to working as a bilingual reporter in the nation's capital. If there was something I had learned during that time, it was that everything was earned through hard work, dedication, consistency, and patience.

U.S. women's national soccer team head coach, Jill Ellis, said it best, "After you climb and get to the top of the mountain, you take it all in and enjoy the moment. You don't dwell on what you've accomplished. Instead, you're looking at which mountain to climb next."

Tackling any mountain requires a commitment to maintaining standards. By adopting certain expectations for myself and always striving to live up to those principles, I created a consistency that allowed me to break through any resistance to come my way. This steadiness has gained me an even stronger faith in myself and the trust of others around me.

But even though I met many obstacles along the way, the commitment and hard work were character lessons that came easy to me. Other lessons had a harder time sinking in, and these lessons would make the greatest impact.

Real growth takes place with patience and consciousness. During and after college, I was sometimes trying to rush to success. I expected everything to move at my speed because my path demanded it. On many occasions, I worked myself to the point of exhaustion and saw nothing in return. This proved to not only be detrimental to my own mindset, but also led me to make some critical mistakes early on in my career.

When I started my career, if I wasn't getting where I wanted to be, when I wanted to be there, it meant that I was going nowhere. The decisions of others were an obstacle or an advancement. If I didn't get the advancement, then I felt stagnant. In reality, my rush to get to the top prevented me from seeing everything that was going on around me.

The Chinese have a parable surrounding the bamboo tree. Someone told me how the Chinese bamboo tree can grow up to ninety feet tall but getting there is a test of character. When the bamboo is planted, it must be nurtured every day to thrive, but it takes years before you get to see the results of your labor. It's easy to give up and believe the time was wasted. But what you don't see are the roots that have been growing underground. All the while building a foundation for the massive tree to come to stand on.

The person who told me this story pointed out that just because I can't see something doesn't mean it isn't there. The roots of my success were growing, and I needed to be patient and aware of everything that was happening. Because our roots don't just come from ourselves but from those around us. I had to learn to consider the reasons I wasn't being allowed to follow the trajectory I wanted. I learned to realize that my superiors were making decisions that affected the lives of others, and I had to respect that regardless of the impact on me. I had to be patient and trust that my consistency and dedication would get me where I needed to be. I had to accept the idea that things would happen on their own. My mother and grandmother call this "*el tiempo de Dios en perfecto*" — God's time is perfect.

After 15 years, I returned to my childhood home on Gramercy Place. This visit gave me the power to close an old chapter in my life and celebrate the vital choices that I made to better my future.

But why am I telling you all this? Because at some point, I believed I wasn't good enough. I spent the early parts of life in an environment that expected nothing from me. So much of my personality came from fighting the belief that I was born to fail. So, when success didn't happen the way I believed it would, it was harder to fight those childhood expectations. Because the parts of my character that came easy to me were hard by nature, I prevented myself from learning the truly hard lessons. It wasn't until I opened my mind and let things happen that I felt like I genuinely deserved success.

I will always continue to nurture my skills and work hard to be the best I can be. But I will also remember that those skills are just one part of a great foundation. A foundation made up of experiences, colleagues, and teachers, but, most importantly, faith, friends, family, and a heritage that all give me the strength to break every barrier that comes my way.

Living the Dream in Tokyo

Allowing the lessons to change my mindset has led my career to an all-time high. I had gone on to win multiple Emmy's producing stories in an array of categories. I continued to meet prominent members of the industry, several that I had admired for years. As the world experienced the effects of the 2020 COVID-19 pandemic, I was lucky enough to be able to use my skills in hopes of making some impact in challenging times. My comprehensive training meant I was well prepared for producing great content from the safety and comfort of my home. This was a change that I accepted with open arms, but it tested my

patience and consciousness. Because prior to the pandemic, I received a phone call that changed my career.

One afternoon, my news director Janette called me and asked if I would be interested in covering the 2020 Summer Olympics in Tokyo, Japan. With my dreams focused on the FIFA World Cup, the Olympics were never something that I had ever considered. Nevertheless, I was thrilled. It was the first time in my career I was being named a correspondent for an event that large and was a big step within my company. The month-long job meant that I would be the national correspondent for all the stations within my company across the country. The dream assignment many work hard for, but very few can obtain. I had been preparing for this big event without knowing it. The World Series, Spring Training, and the Stanley Cup were all great lessons about what to expect.

The COVID-19 outbreak meant the games would be postponed until 2021. But despite the delay, it will never take away from how good it felt to be a part of this. When the phone call came in, I was standing next to my mother as if it was destiny. Seconds after hanging up the phone, we embraced each other in joy, but I couldn't contain my emotions as I began to weep. I remembered everything I had endured for years when no one would take a chance on me. As I wiped my tears, my mother grabbed me by the shoulders and told me how proud she was of all of my hard work.

I asked myself what would've happened if I had decided to quit when things weren't going as I expected. That question alone helped me realize that I was exactly where I needed to be. This is still just the beginning for me. I want that to be an inspiration for youths and people of color all around the country. So, you can tell yourself, this is only the beginning. You will make it.

Tokyo Olympics

About the Author

Moisés Linares currently resides in Virginia, just five minutes away from the nation's capital. Still working in sports journalism, he holds a position as a bilingual sports reporter in Washington D.C.

The year 2021 began a new chapter in his career as he juggled being a Spanish TV play-by-play announcer for D.C. United while holding a radio gig with the Washington Football Team.

When not working, Moisés enjoys travelling and exploring all the beauty the U.S. has to offer. For the past few years, he's been honing his skills as a public speaker, often recording motivational videos and visiting schools virtually and in-person.

Though *We Are Not Born Failures* is Moisés first book, his future plans include composing a sports documentary and possibly writing a second book.

Made in the USA
Columbia, SC
11 April 2022

58585345R00134